Guide to the

New Mexico Mountains

Guide to the
New Mexico Mountains

Herbert E. Ungnade

UNIVERSITY OF NEW MEXICO PRESS

Albuquerque

To my wife
PAULINA

TABLE OF CONTENTS

THE CLIMBING GUIDE

TABLE OF MAPS AND DIAGRAMS

TABLE OF PHOTOGRAPHS

MOUNTAIN RANGES IN NEW MEXICO
AND COUNTIES IN WHICH THEY ARE LOCATED

Mountain Range	*County*
Animas Mountains	Hidalgo
Bear Mountains	Socorro
Big Burro Mountains	Grant
Big Hatchet Mountains	Hidalgo
Black Range	Grant, Sierra
Brazos Mountains	Rio Arriba
Broke Off Mountains	Otero
Caballo Mountains	Sierra
Capitan Mountains	Lincoln
Cebolleta Mountains	McKinley, Sandoval
Cedar Mountain Range	Luna
Chupadera Mountains	Socorro
Chuska Mountains	McKinley, San Juan
Cooks Range	Luna
Cornudas Mountains	Otero
Datil Mountains	Catron
Diablo Range	Catron, Grant
Doña Ana Mountains	Doña Ana
Elk Mountains	Catron
Florida Mountains	Luna
Fra Cristobal Range	Sierra
Franklin Mountains	Doña Ana
Gallinas Mountains	Lincoln
Gallinas Mountains	Socorro
Gallo Mountains	Catron
Guadalupe Mountains	Eddy, Otero
Jarilla Mountains	Otero
Jemez Mountains	Rio Arriba, Sandoval

Jerky Mountains	Catron
Jicarilla Mountains	Lincoln
Kelly Mountains	Catron
Ladron Mountains	Socorro
Lemitar Mountains	Socorro
Little Burro Mountains	Grant
Little Hatchet Mountains	Hidalgo
Long Canyon Mountains	Catron
Los Pinos Mountains	Socorro
Luera Mountains	Catron
Magdalena Mountains	Socorro
Mangas Mountains	Catron
Manzano Mountains	Bernalillo, Torrance
Mimbres Mountains	Grant, Sierra
Mogollon Mountains	Catron
Mule Mountains	Grant
Organ Mountains	Doña Ana
Ortiz Mountains	Santa Fe
Oscura Mountains	Lincoln, Socorro
Peloncillo Mountains	Hidalgo
Picacho-Robledo Mountains	Doña Ana
Pinos Altos Mountains	Grant
Potrillo Mountains	Doña Ana
Pyramid Mountains	Hidalgo
Sacramento Mountains	Otero
Saliz Mountains	Catron
San Andres Mountains	Doña Ana, Sierra
San Augustin Mountains	Doña Ana
Sandia Mountains	Bernalillo, Sandoval
San Francisco Mountains	Catron
Sangre de Cristo Mountains	Colfax, Mora, Rio Arriba, San Miguel, Santa Fe, Taos
San Mateo Mountains	Socorro
San Mateo Mountains	Valencia
San Pedro Mountains	Rio Arriba
San Pedro Mountains	Santa Fe

Sawtooth Mountains	Catron
Sierra Blanca	Lincoln, Otero
Sierra de las Uvas	Doña Ana
Sierra Nacimiento	Sandoval
Sierra Rica	Hidalgo
Socorro Mountains	Socorro
Tres Hermanas	Luna
Tularosa	Catron
Victorio Mountains	Luna
Zuni Mountains	McKinley, Valencia

STATE PARKS

Alamogordo Lake	De Baca
Bluewater Lake	Valencia
Bottomless Lakes	Chaves
Caballo Lake	Sierra
City of Rocks	Grant
Clayton Lake	Union
Conchas Lake	San Miguel
El Vado Lake	Rio Arriba
Elephant Butte Lake	Sierra
Fort Selden	Doña Ana
Hyde Memorial	Santa Fe
Kit Carson Memorial	Taos
Morphy Lake	Mora
Navajo Lake	Rio Arriba, San Juan
Oasis	Roosevelt
Pancho Villa	Luna
Rio Grande Gorge	Taos
Rock Hound	Grant
Santa Fe River	Santa Fe
Storrie Lake	San Miguel
Ute Lake	Quay
Valley of Fires	Lincoln
Villanueva	San Miguel

STATE MONUMENTS

Abo	Torrance
Coronado	Sandoval
El Palacio (Palace of the Governors)	Santa Fe
Folsom	Colfax
Gran Quivira	Torrance
Jemez	Sandoval
La Mesilla	Doña Ana
Lincoln County	Lincoln
Paako	Bernalillo
Pecos	San Miguel
Quarai	Torrance

WILDERNESS AND WILD AREAS

Name	*Forest*
Black Range Primitive Area	Gila
Blue Range Primitive Area	Apache
Gila Primitive Area	Gila
Gila Wilderness Area	Gila
Pecos Wilderness Area	Carson, Santa Fe
San Pedro Parks Wild Area	Santa Fe
Wheeler Peak Wild Area	Carson
White Mountain Wild Area	Lincoln

NATIONAL PARK

Carlsbad Caverns	Eddy County

NATIONAL MONUMENTS

Name	County
Aztec Ruins	San Juan
Bandelier	Sandoval
Capulin Mountain	Union
Chaco Canyon	San Juan
El Morro (Inscription Rock)	Valencia
Fort Union	Mora
Gila Cliff Dwellings	Catron
Gran Quivira	Torrance
Pecos	San Miguel
White Sands	Doña Ana, Otero

NATIONAL FORESTS

Name	County
Apache	Catron
Carson	Rio Arriba, Taos
Cibola	Bernalillo, Catron, Lincoln, McKinley, Sandoval, Socorro, Torrance, Valencia
Coronado	Hidalgo
Gila	Catron, Grant, Sierra
Lincoln	Chaves, Eddy, Lincoln, Otero
Santa Fe	Mora, Rio Arriba, Sandoval, San Miguel, Santa Fe

MOUNTAIN RANGES OF NEW MEXICO

INTRODUCTION

It often comes as a surprise to strangers to learn that New Mexico has mountains, but there are actually few places in the state where some mountains are not visible.

Starting from the Colorado State Line, the ranges run mainly north and south across the state and beyond its borders into Texas and Mexico. The high peaks in the northern part of the state which rise above 13,000' are covered with snow during much of the year, although the snowfields shrink to little patches by the end of summer. The high peaks are surrounded by dense forest in wilderness areas and drained by old glacial gorges with lakes and waterfalls. They have steep cliffs with exciting routes for climbing. Above 12,000' one finds tundra with tiny alpine flowers in brilliant colors. The high country is quite cool and may have snow flurries even in summer; storms come up suddenly and the winds rarely stop blowing on the high ridges. These mountains are therefore not much different from the slightly higher uplifts farther north.

There are miles of mountain ridges along the Rio Grande River, the Tularosa Basin, and the Plains of San Augustin, and numerous volcanic necks from the famous Shiprock to the virtually unknown Alesna.

Southern New Mexico has mountains of lower altitude which rise from barren desert, where cactus and rattlesnake rival lack of water for hazard.

While there is a general trend for decreasing altitude in going from north to south, the profile of the mountains, or the elevation difference from base to summit, does not decrease in the same way, and several southern ranges rise more than 5,000' above their valleys.

Exploration of the mountain regions of New Mexico began at the end of the 19th century; until then it was undisputed Indian territory. Mountaineering is much more recent. Climbers and hikers were preceded by explorers, prospectors, surveyors, hunters, and trappers. Only when roads and trails were pushed into the wilderness within the last 40 years did the mountains become really accessible.

Mountain and hiking clubs throughout the state have helped to popularize the mountains by organizing trips and climbs. The Los Alamos Mountaineers have maintained registers on some major peaks including Wheeler Peak, three of the Truchas Peaks, Santa Fe Baldy, and, for a time, Lake Peak. Yet there is no guidebook to the high country.

The present volume was begun as a guide to the Sangre de Cristo Mountains, with which the author is long familiar. When it was decided to include the entire mountain areas of the state, trail and route information was solicited from the Los Alamos Mountaineers, Los Alamos Outdoor Association, New Mexico Mountaineers, Southwestern Mountaineers, National Park Service, U. S. Forest Service, and U. S. Geological Survey, to whom the author is indebted. Special acknowledgments are due to George Bell, Norman Bullard, Kenneth Ewing, James Fretwell, Ingraham, who helped with climbing information, and Ernest Anderson, Harold Butler, Robert Harris, Laurence Campbell, and Donald Liska.

This book is written primarily for the climber and hiker, but a chapter is included describing roads through and up the mountains for those who wish to view them close by automobile or jeep.

The book is intended to give trail and road information into the best known mountain ranges of New Mexico. It starts the reader from a place which can be readily found on a road map and sends him on a route into a particular mountain area. Distances in some cases are estimates, based in part on road maps or Forest Service figures and in part on personal measurements and hiking trips. Many of the suggested routes have been checked by the author.

The general maps which appear in the text show roads and mountain ranges for orientation purposes. More detailed maps contain streams and creeks, as well as the main roads and trails. Altitudes of mountains have been compiled from U.S.G.S. data, as much as possible from the most recent surveys.

If errors are found or if better routes or later data become known, the author should be pleased to be informed. It is hoped that the guidebook can be kept up-to-date and as complete as possible.

Geological History

New Mexico offers not only a wide variety of geological features but also a complete record of geological history from Precambrian rocks to Alluvium. In a given region some periods may be missing because they were removed by erosion or failed to be deposited, but every geological age is represented somewhere in the state. The complexity of the mountain ridges is due to two different periods of folding and considerable volcanic activity at different times during the long geological past. In ancient times the region of New Mexico contained seas which deposited marine sediments. Powerful compressive forces squeezed the land from north and south, building up high east-west mountain ranges and converting sedimentary rocks into metamorphic varieties such as quartzite and mica schist. Intrusions of magma and hot silicate solutions formed granite and quartz veins, some of them with valuable metallic ores. The northern part of New Mexico remained above sea level for a long time during the Paleozoic period until the Mississippian age when a sea washed over the lower land. Erosion debris from the quartzite ridges washed into the sea and was deposited as a sedimentary layer directly on the Precambrian rocks. Where this is the case, as for instance in the Sangre de Cristo Mountains, the early Paleozoic formations are missing. The resulting gap is referred to as the "Great Unconformity."

Southern New Mexico, on the other hand, was submerged during much of the Paleozoic era and received deposits of marine sediments which became sandstone, limestone, and shale. Deposits of Mississippian sandstone and limestone are found distributed over the entire state, as are the sedimentary rocks of the Pennsylvanian age which followed, since most of the state remained under water during these periods. Most of the older sedimentary rocks date from the Pennsylvanian era, which left irregular deposits reaching up to 8,000' in thickness. Much smaller layers of red shale and sandstone were formed during the Permian age, but during this period the great deposits of salt, gypsum, and potash were laid down in southeastern New Mexico.

Near the end of the Mesozoic period which followed, tremendous forces slowly pushed the earth's crust into north-south folds. This so-called Laramide Revolution created north-south mountain ranges over much of the state along extensive fault zones. Simultaneous sinking of other blocks created depressions such as the Rio Grande Valley. The high country was not submerged again after this time but was further molded by erosion. During the last glaciation the high peaks had small glaciers which carved the typical U-shaped valleys and cirques of the higher mountain ranges as far south as Sierra Blanca. Other parts of the state were submerged during the Cretaceous period and received further marine deposits. Near the end of this period the land rose again, and the accumulated vegetation gave rise to coal beds. The most important Cenozoic event was the intrusion and extrusion of magmas.

The geology of the mountains was first described by the surveyor Hayden in 1869, the Wheeler surveyors in 1875-81, and later by members of the U. S. Geological Survey and other geologists who became interested in New Mexico. A number of the more recent accounts have been published by the New Mexico Geological Societies and the Bureau of Mines and Mineral Resources at the School of Mines in Socorro.

Archaeological History

Evidence of the earliest human occupation of the mountain regions in New Mexico comes from Sandia Cave, located in the Sandia Mountains below Palomas Peak, at an altitude of 7,000'. The bottom layer of this cave contained crudely-flaked spear points and bones of prehistoric horse, bison, camel, mastodon, and mammoth, dated at 25,000-26,000 years ago and preceding the last major glaciation in the Pleistocene era. During the humid period which followed the cave was closed and deposits of yellow ochre were laid down over the Sandia layer. A layer above this false floor contained bones of extinct species of horse and sloth, together with the characteristic centergrooved projectile points assigned to the Folsom period of 10,000 years ago.

Folsom man roamed over much of the region adjacent to the mountains. Fluted points have been found at Folsom (after which the culture is named), near Las Vegas, south of Ojo Caliente, in ancient buffalo wallows in the San Luis Valley, near Clovis, from plains to foothills in Socorro County, in the Plains of San Augustin, as far south as Burnet Cave in the Guadalupe Mountains, and in Mexico. The age of this culture was established from geological evidence and from the association of artifacts with extinct species which can be dated. Thus, in Deadhorse Gulch near Folsom a fluted point was discovered between the ribs of an extinct species of bison, the Bison Taylori of the late Pleistocene.

In southwestern New Mexico the early hunters were followed by a culture called Cochise, which began over 10,000 years ago and depended chiefly on food gathering rather than hunting. In the Socorro region this culture is represented by numerous sites in plains, river terraces, and canyons, in the foothills and on the high ridges and saddles of the mountains. These campsites contained crude hearths, milling stones and manos, chips, flakes, knives, choppers, and scrapers. The Cochise may be the ancestors of the Mogollon people who appeared in central and western New Mexico around the beginning of the Christian era. The Mogollon were hunters and fishermen and lived in the mountains after which they are named, although their remains have been found over a much larger area. On various changes in their sites, it has been possible to distinguish several phases of the Mogollon period. The last of these is a distinctive culture which thrived in the Mimbres Valley beginning around 1,000 A.D. and is referred to as the Mimbres Phase. These people buried pottery with their dead and left in this fashion some of the most beautiful and interesting bowls ever made. The people disappeared from the fertile valley in the twelfth century.

Meanwhile in northern New Mexico and elsewhere in the southwest a new culture appeared which is called collectively the Anasazi (Navajo, the ancient ones) culture and includes Basketmaker and Pueblo. The Basketmakers presumably came from the north some 2,000 years ago or earlier and eventually spread over the entire state of New Mexico, where they assimilated the Mogollon. The resulting Pueblo culture is usually dated from 700 A.D. and continues to the present day. There are numerous remains of Basketmaker and Pueblo Indians and it is possible to follow their cultural development from the early preceramic stage through developmental stages to the Classic or Great-Pueblo period of large communities with much specialization and high development of art and architecture, which left such ruins as Mesa Verde, Chaco Canyon, and Kayenta. It is during this "golden period" of the Anasazi at about 1,000-1,300 A.D. that Navajo and Apache tribes first drifted into the southwest from regions farther north. The decline of the Anasazi culture coincides with the great drought at the end of the thirteenth century (1276-1300), aided perhaps by raids from these nomadic Indians. A smaller population survived in the Rio Grande drainage of New Mexico, represented by Regressive-Pueblo sites such as Puye and Tyuonyi, which are said to be the ancestral homes of the present-day Pueblos.

When the Pleistocene hunters migrated south, the high country in New Mexico was glaciated and their campsites are found at elevations below 8,000'. As the ice receded, hunters gradually ventured into the higher reaches, and in the period of 3,000 to

1,500 years ago hunting parties camped even on the high passes at 10,000-12,000'. Numerous artifacts have been collected from more than a dozen campsites. There is good evidence that the high ridges were crossed by hunting parties during the Pueblo period. Moreover, during this time many of the major summits were climbed and shrines were established which were visited continuously until historic times.

Recorded History

The Coronado Expedition of 1540 explored Zuni, the northern Rio Grande Valley from Tiguex (near the present town of Bernalillo) as far as Taos, and the buffalo plains, crossing the mountains east and west of Cicuye (Pecos). Forty years later, Augustin Rodriguez brough a much smaller missionary expedition from Chihuahua up the Rio Grande to Puaray (near Bernalillo). He remained there with Francisco Lopez, and both were martyred. The expedition of Espejo and Beltran in 1582-83 was undertaken to ascertain the fate of the Franciscans at Puaray. The group explored the Pueblo country and returned by a new route down the Pecos River. After this time, the country north of Mexico was called Nuevo Mejico.

The first successful attempt at colonization in the region was Don Juan de Oñate's expedition of 1598, which was equipped at his own expense and entered the territory at El Paso del Norte (now Juarez). The colonists moved up the Rio Grande and settled at San Gabriel, the first capital, which was moved to Santa Fe under Governor Peralta in 1610. During the 17th century, Spanish haciendas extended from Taos to Isleta. It was a period of intense missionary effort, but there was also considerable exploitation of the Indians in the form of tributes and forced labor, both by the friars and by the governors. This led to the Pueblo Revolt during the term of Governor Otermin in 1680 which forced the abandonment of the province. The colonists fled south to the present site of El Paso.

The reconquest of New Mexico under Don Diego de Vargas

took place thirteen years later. Colonists resettled the Rio Grande Valley, the missions were reestablished, and there followed a period of uneasy coexistence between Spanish and Indians, particularly Apache and Comanche, with many raids on both sides. Drought, famine, and smallpox in 1780 added to the hardships; but the small colony survived in a remote region, almost unknown to the outside world. Lt. Zebulon Pike's expedition in 1807 brought to the United States the first information about the Spanish territory of New Mexico. During the remaining years of Spanish rule, New Mexico was carefully guarded against foreign intruders. The borders were opened only when Mexico gained independence from Spain in 1821.

The Santa Fe Trail became a busy trade route, and mountain men such as Pattie, Ceran St. Vrain, Antoine Robidoux, and Kit Carson trapped beaver along the little streams in the mountains. Land grants made during this time created the vast Spanish land holdings which still exist in parts of New Mexico and Colorado.

New Mexico was occupied in bloodless conquest by the Army of the West under General Kearny in 1846. The only serious resistance, the Taos Pueblo Revolt in 1847, was put down by Colonel Price. The treaty of Guadalupe Hidalgo with Mexico in 1848 ceded New Mexico to the United States. The new territory of the United States was explored by various military reconnaissances from 1848 to 1857. During this time the Indian depredations made it necessary to establish a series of frontier forts to protect the settlers, who entered the territory in increasing numbers. The Indians were gradually settled on reservations or subdued, not, however, without considerable violence.

The Civil War saw only minor skirmishes in New Mexico. The Confederates were beaten by the Union troops near Glorieta at the southern end of the Sangre de Cristo Mountains. With the end of the war and the settling of the Indians on reservations came intensive explorations of the mountains by prospectors and a mining boom which was to last for a decade or more. During these years the mountains were surveyed, first by Hayden and then by the groups under Lt. Wheeler; many of the summits were given English names, and the first accurate descriptions and maps of the mountains were issued by the new U. S. Geological Survey (founded 1879). The first railroad inside the Territory crossed Raton Pass in 1878.

This was the time of open range, cattle empires, cattle wars, overgrazing, and gully cutting. The vast forests in the northern mountains were cut in annual tie drives, when more than a quarter million railroad ties were floated down the Rio Grande, to fill the growing demands of the railroads. Forest fires destroyed thousands of acres of timber, and far-sighted men pushed legislation for the protection of the watersheds.

Since the beginning of the twentieth century most of the high country has come under the management of the U.S. Forest Service. Erosion control is beginning to check the damage done in the past. Wildlife has been restored in many regions and the forests are now preserved under the multiple use program. The major change in the mountains has been an increase in the number of roads, ski areas, radio and television towers. Some of the most beautiful regions in the western mountains have been protected against such inroads by the creation of wilderness, primitive, and wild areas, and recent legislation has secured these areas for future generations.

Climate and Vegetation

Six of the seven known life (or climatic) zones are found in New Mexico. Only the tropical zone does not occur in the state. The altitudes of the land vary from 2,876' to 13,160' and there is a drop of roughly 3°F for every 1,000' increase in altitude. Simultaneously the amount of annual precipitation varies from 8-10'' at 3,000-4,500' to 20-30'' at 7,000-9,000'. Depending on the approximate altitude, the following life zones can be distinguished:

Lower Sonoran		3,000-5,000'
Upper Sonoran		5,000-7,000'
Transition	} (Montane)	7,000-8,000'
Canadian		8,000-10,000'

Hudsonian   (Subalpine)   10,000-12,000'
Arctic Alpine (Alpine)   12,000-13,000'

Each of these zones has distinctive plants and animals, and one
can choose different climate and surroundings in New Mexico
simply by changing altitude. The habitat of various plants, however, depends also on soil, exposure, and humidity, and the altitudes are therefore approximate.

The warmest zone in the state, the Lower Sonoran, is found
in the lower Rio Grande Valley (Rio Abajo), the Deming Plain,
and the Tularosa Basin. The predominant plants (zone indicat-
ors) are grama grass, mesquite, creosote bush, and several cactus
(Opuntia) and yucca species. The widespread yucca is the state
flower of New Mexico. The Upper Sonoran, along the Rio
Arriba or upper Rio Grande, has characteristic juniper and
piñon pine growth and buffalo grass. It contains some of the most
valuable grazing and ranching land, and also thousands of acres of
sagebrush. Cottonwood trees are found along the rivers and irrigation ditches.

The Transition zone is recognized by the large forests of ponderosa pine (yellow pine) which include much of the timber
reserves in the state. There are also varieties of oak, willow,
maple, birch, locust, wild plum, and cherry in this zone. Bushes
such as currant, gooseberry, buckthorn, wild rose, and snowberry
furnish the undergrowth, and kinnikinnic spreads a green carpet
on the rocky forest floor. This is the habitat for deer, black bear,
wildcat, coyote, wild turkey, grouse, and many song birds.

The main trees in the Canadian zone are Douglas fir and
quaking aspen. In the fall of the year, forests of aspen turn yellow, and in places red, and the zone can be recognized without
difficulty. Meadows in this zone may have Mariposa lilies, irises,
Colorado blue columbines, gentians, and daisies.

Englemann spruce, bristlecone (foxtail) pine, cork-barked fir,
and limber pine mark the onset of the Hudsonian zone below
timberline. This region receives the heaviest snowfall and is
sometimes called the snow zone. Abundant moisture gives it lux-

uriant vegetation. Subalpine meadows contain elephantella, bistort, rose crown, paint brush, and pearly everlasting; the spruce forest contains twin flower, lady slipper, and fairy slipper. Along the streams will be found the chiming bell, monkshood, Parry primrose, arnica, and larkspur. This zone represents the sheep-grazing region of the mountains. Timberline starts in the upper elevations of this zone. The combined forces of wind and snow produce a forest of extraordinary quality at this altitude. Some trees are grotesquely twisted with branches only on the lee side. Others hug the ground, growing in the shelter of rocks or hollows in the ground. Gradually the trees become smaller and then there is only tundra.

The mountain region above timberline is known as the Arctic Alpine zone, and consists of grasslands, meadows, rock fields, and cliffs. On the high meadows are found alpine sunflowers (Rydbergia) and marsh marigolds, large cushions of moss campion, and innumerable dwarf flowers in the most brilliant colors. Among these are forget-me-nots, dwarf primroses and gentians. The rocks beyond the last tundra are often covered with colorful lichens.

Wildlife

From all accounts it appears that Indians and Spanish did little to affect the wildlife population in New Mexico. Despite the annual buffalo hunts by nearly all of the Indian tribes since ancient times, the buffalo (bison) survived in the plains until almost the turn of the century. There was little hunting done by the Spaniards. The first groups of travelers on the Santa Fe Trail reported that the woods were full of game, the plains and canyons full of antelope and buffalo, and the streams teeming with fish. There were more beavers than people, and wolves were so numerous that burials had to be covered with rocks. Lt. W. H. Emory encountered grizzly bears, elks, turkeys, and ducks in 1848. He describes herds of hundreds of antelope in canyons south of Raton Pass. As late as 1895 Prof. L. L. Dyche of the University of Kansas found much game in the Sangre de Cristo Mountains. He was then collecting specimens for the Kansas University Museum, as some species were in danger of extinction. There appears to have been little thought of conservation in those days. Everyone hunted at will, and hide hunters roamed the hills. It is not surprising, therefore, that some species disappeared. Among these were the buffalo, the native elk (extinct around 1900), grizzly bear, and Rocky Mountain bighorn sheep. Black bear, deer, antelope, mountain lion, and coyote survived. Elk (Cervus canadenis nelsoni) were reintroduced in the Sangre de Cristo Mountains in 1915, bighorn sheep in the Sandias. Wild turkeys, quail, and pheasants have been replaced in sections where they were killed out. Fish from the state fish hatcheries are being planted in most streams and lakes. With game refuges and regulated hunting seasons, most of the present game animals have an excellent chance to hold their own. Only some predators, such as mountain lions, wolves, and bobcats, are now in danger of becoming extinct. Coyotes are quite common. Beavers, which were nearly extinct in 1830, have come back, and it is once again possible to see their dams and lodges in the mountain valleys. Porcupines have become so numerous in some regions that they damage much of the conifer growth. Skunks can be seen (and smelled) quite frequently on the Pajarito Plateau in the Jemez Mountains and occur in almost all parts of the state. The western red fox is native to the Jemez and Sangre de Cristo Mountains. The once common prairie dogs are seen seldom. They have been almost eliminated because they were harmful to crops. The high country abounds in rodents of various kinds, including ground squirrels, packrats, chipmunks, and squirrels at lower altitudes; and conies (Ochotona princeps saxatilis) above timberline. The playful marmots (Marmota flaviventris luteola) can be seen at all high altitudes, although they are more numerous in the subalpine zone in the Sangre de Cristo Mountains.

Grouse and wild turkeys are sometimes scared up in the woods, and on the high tundra one can see occasionally ptarmigans whose plumage matches rocks in the summer and snow in the winter.

Hawks, ravens, and eagles soar in the skies. The black and white Rocky Mountain magpies can be seen along the mountain roads, and picknickers and campers are familiar with the Canada jay, commonly called camp robber, because he will gather around campgrounds and pick up scraps. Water ouzels and juncos are at home in the high country. The state bird of New Mexico, the crested road runner, is usually seen at lower altitudes trying to outrun horses and cars. Throughout the seasons some 300 species of birds of almost all climatic zones in the state can be found in the mountains.

Reptiles are more plentiful in the warmer climate of the lower altitudes in central and southern New Mexico. One can find numerous snakes, lizards, toads, and turtles in this region. Rattlesnakes occur throughout the state, but are seldom found at altitudes above 7,000'. The poisonous Gila monsters are rare in New Mexico, but many species of harmless lizards can be found in almost all climates. Horned toads are widely distributed. Tarantulas, which have a horrid appearance, are relatively harmless, but the bite of the tiny Black Widow spider can be deadly.

Mineral Resources

The Spanish expedition of 1540 into what is now New Mexico was undertaken in search of gold (the Seven Cities of Cibola), but it found little more than salt and some turquoise. Later expeditions went through the Rio Grande and Pecos valleys past ore deposits which would have made them all rich beyond their fondest dreams; however, they followed their Indian guides along the streams and avoided the hostile heights.

In the nearly 300 years of Spanish rule, few mines were worked. There was much prospecting, and there is evidence that gold was found in small quantities, along with silver, copper, and lead. Spanish diggings, ore samples, or smelters have been found around Pedernal, in the Sandias, Manzanos, Jemez and Ladrones, at Cerillos, and in the Ortiz and Socorro Mountains. After the Pueblo Revolt, some of these mines were hidden by the Indians, so successfully that they have not been found to date. Few made any real profits. The Spanish preoccupation with mining is apparent from the discovery in 1867 that El Palacio, the governor's palace in Santa Fe, contained a smelting furnace worn from long and hard usage.

The only successful mine in Spanish times was the Santa Rita, which shipped 20,000 mule loads of copper by mule trains to Chihuahua. The operation started in 1804, near the end of the Spanish regime. The major finds under the Republic of Mexico (1821-1846) were gold-bearing gravels in the Ortiz and San Pedro Mountains. When New Mexico became a territory of the United States, various military groups made geological observations and some valuable ores were found. The mining operations which were started were soon interrupted by the Confederate invasion of 1862 and numerous Indian raids.

The years shortly after the war are marked by the discovery of gold near Nogal and in Moreno Valley, and lead-silver ore near Magdalena. This was followed later by the silver strikes around Silver City and in Lake Valley. The railroad came in 1878 and made various mining ventures more profitable. About 1890 there was a mining boom in various parts of New Mexico which lasted for a decade or more. Almost every mountain range in the state was found to contain some kind of useful mineral.

The mining of turquoise probably antedates any other kind of mining in the United States. Prehistoric workings and stone tools have been found near Cerrillos, in the Burro Mountains, near Old Hachita, and in the Jarillas. Turquoise was excavated from a Basketmaker III site in Chaco Canyon, tentatively dated at 700 A.D. It was found in amazing quantities in burials at Pueblo Bonito, dated about 1000 A.D., and is believed to have originated from the extensive prehistoric mining operations at Mount Chalchihuitl, 2.5 miles north of Cerrillos. The ancient diggings were rediscovered and worked in part after the middle of the last century. Some turquoise was probably mined in the Cerrillos district during Spanish times, but there are not even estimates for the amounts taken out. The Cerrillos production between 1890 and

1900 was worth at least several million dollars. After turquoise was rediscovered in the Burro Mountains in 1875, the mines there yielded even more turquoise than the Cerrillos district. Ancient workings near Old Hachita were discovered in 1878, and the mines were reopened in 1885. Turquoise deposits at Orogrande were developed in 1898.

Gold mining is possibly the most exciting mining activity because one associates visions of great riches with gold. The placer gold mines in the Ortiz Mountains were most likely the first in the United States. Both old and new placers in the adjacent San Pedro Mountains yielded gold, and even now some metal is found, but the rich mother lode has not been rediscovered to date. The gold discovery of 1866 in the Cimarron Range led to a wild mining boom which eventually exhausted the ore. Many copper and silver mines in the state contained a percentage of gold as minor constituents, but others had nearly pure gold, both in placers and lodes. Among these was the White Oaks district discovered by Baxter, Winters, and Wilson. The Old Abe mine near White Oaks produced some three million dollars worth of gold. Other gold mines were located in the Hillsboro district in Sierra County, in the Organ, Socorro, and Lemitar Mountains, and at Pinos Altos.

Silver was found in such quantity in New Mexico that one city, Silver City, was named for this mineral. It occurred in the Black Hawk, Burro Mountain, Central, Chloride Flat, Eureka, Fleming, Georgetown, Gold Hill, Lone Mountain, Pinos Altos, Santa Rita, and White Signal districts in Grant County. The ore in the Hawk mine at Bullard Peak was almost pure silver extending for 20 to 25 feet from the surface. The richest body of silver ore, worth three million dollars, was found in the Bridal Chamber near Lake Valley in 1884, shortly after the mine was sold for $100,000. Native silver came from the Silver Cell mine in the Pinos Altos district in 1891. There were several silver mines in the Organs and elsewhere, but the silver producers closed down in 1893 when silver was demonetized.

The history of copper mining in the state has been long and

involved. The rich Santa Rita near Silver City was worked by Indians in prehistoric times and reopened by the Spaniards in 1804. It became later a large open-pit mine. In stripping various sections, old fills with timbers and skeletons have been discovered, dating back to Indian, Spanish, Mexican, and more recent times. Copper was mined in the Sierra Nacimiento, in the Organs, and in the Terrero Mine near Pecos.

Zinc occuring as sphalerite (ZnS) was the chief mineral in the Magdalena district. Stream tin has been found in the Black Range. By far one of the most important metals, however, is the molybdenum of the "Moly" in Red River Canyon near Questa. First mistaken for graphite, this deposit of high-grade disulfide (MoS_2) is one of the three largest known molybdenum deposits in the world.

The most recent mining boom concerns the uranium finds at Haystack Mountain near Grants. It occurs widespread in the Todilto limestone and in the sandstones of the Morrisson formation.

Abundant occurrence of muscovite (mica) led to the use of this material as windowglass in early Santa Fe. Muscovite is still mined in the Petaca district.

Among the most important non-metallic minerals in New Mexico are the potash deposits in the Permian Basin in the southeastern part of the state, fluorspar in the southern mountains, and coal in northern New Mexico.

EXPLORING THE HIGH COUNTRY

The First Mountaineers

There is extensive evidence that the prehistoric Indians were the first mountaineers. Our knowledge of their explorations is based on archaeological findings and legends of the surviving Indian tribes. There are few or no artifacts from the higher elevations which can be traced definitely to the earliest cultures such as Sandia or Folsom Man. This is understandable, as the high country was glaciated during part of this time. The findings in the mountains belong to the later periods of the pre-ceramic hunters and gatherers of 3,000 to 1,500 years ago or earlier. The sites at higher altitudes probably represent summer camps. There is evidence of later occupations of high ridges and summits, particularly during the Pueblo Period, not only for hunting but also for religious purposes.

The mountains were the source of all water in this arid country, and it is not suprising that the primitive people regarded them as the dwelling places of the deities and built shrines on their summits. Springs, lakes, and mountains were held sacred and became the sites of special ceremonies. For reasons of their own, the present day Indians have been exceedingly reticent to tell about shrines on mountains and are very vague about their existence. It is known that Sierra Blanca was sacred to the ancient Indians as well as the more recent Apache, who have settled nearby. Magdalena Peak west of Socorro was also sacred. The hot springs in various parts of the state were frequently visited and the areas around them were respected as sanctuaries.

The Pueblo Indians usually had mountains in the four directions of the compass and a number of sacred hills as well. The Tewas (San Juan, Santa Clara, and San Ildefonso) had in addition at least three other mountains representing zenith, nadir, and the center of all. The mountain of the north was Keping (Bear Mountain), the present San Antonio Peak on Highway 285 near the Colorado State Line. Okuping (Turtle Mountain) = Sandia Mountain was the mountain of the south; Tsikupuming (Obsidian Mountain) = Cerro Pelado, the mountain of the west; and Kuseping (Blue Stone Mountain), the present Lake Peak, the mountain of the east. The former shrines on the tops of these mountains have been destroyed, and we have only statements to the effect that they existed. Tschicoma (Tsikomo) was regarded as the "Center of All," not only by the Tewas but also by other tribes. The shrine on its summit was described by W. B. Douglass, who climbed the peak in 1911. It was an elliptical enclosure with seven exits pointing to Taos, San Juan, Santa Clara, San Ildefonso, Jemez, Cochiti, and the Navajo (?) region. A depression in the focal point held a vase altar with prayer sticks. The summit was marked by a mound of stones 10′ in diameter, 5′ high, and with a spruce pole in the center 8′ high. A shrine of rectangular shape was seen by Douglass in the same year on top of Redondo some 16 miles distant. In this case a mound of stones 10′ in diameter and 4′ high was observed on the east side of the summit. It is said that the shrine was visited each year in August by the Indians of Jemez, Zia, Santa Domingo, Sandia, Cochiti, San Ildefonso, Santa Clara, and San Juan.

The mountain southeast of Picuris, now called Jicarita, was sacred to the Picuris, who maintained a shrine on its summit. The Picuris Indians probably visited other summits in the region and were seen in the Santa Barbara drainage basin within recent times.

Pueblo Peak north of Taos was the sacred mountain of the Taos Indians, who called it Maxwaluna. It is still in the sacred area including Blue Lake, which is now within the Taos Indian Special Use Area of Carson National Forest. The area is closed to the public and requires a special permit to enter.

Three of the sacred mountains of the Navajos—Shiprock, Mount Taylor and Cabezon—are volcanic in origin. The latter two were climbed by the Indians, and Cabezon still has a shrine on its summit. While many of the Indian shrines could be reached by trails, the Indians evidently did not hesitate to climb the rocks if this were the only way to the top, as is the case for Cabezon and Pedernal.

As far as is known, the Spaniards did not climb mountains in New Mexico unless one can consider the epic climb of the rock of Acoma by Vicente de Zaldivar in this category. It is probably safe to say that only Indians climbed the summits before 1820. The mountain men who went after beaver explored the high country thereafter, and they were followed by the military expeditions, prospectors, miners, and surveyors.

Mountain Roads

One cannot drive any great distance in New Mexico without driving over mountains or along mountain ranges. Many mountains have roads to the summits, some built for sightseeing, others as service roads for mines, fire lookouts, a few laboratories, and communications or television installations. Most of these roads are open to the public, and at many lookouts visitors are welcome. Scenic trips on such roads are described in the following, grouped according to regions.

Northeastern New Mexico

If one enters New Mexico from Trinidad, Colorado, on U.S. 85, the state line is crossed on the north side of Raton Pass (7,834'). The pass is not far from the location of the toll road which Dick Wootton built over the pass in 1866. The Santa Fe Railroad uses a tunnel on the west side below the pass. The top of the pass gives magnificent views into Colorado to the north, and over the plains, mesas, and mountains of New Mexico to the south. The northeast corner of the state is an area of former volcanic activity which left large sheets of lava and more than one hundred extinct volcanoes. To see more of the volcanic area, take State Road 72 east from Raton to Folsom and Capulin. East of Raton (Spanish, rat), 6,600', the road climbs Manco Burro Pass and tops out on Johnson Mesa, 19 miles east of Raton. From here one can see a skyline rimmed with ancient volcanoes such as Red Mountain, Jose Butte, Capulin Mountain, Sierra Grande, Robinson Mountain, Malpais Mountain, Horseshoe Mountain, Palo Blanco, Timber Butte, and Laughlin Peak. The basalt covered Johnson Mesa has a spring and rich soil. It was settled in 1887 by Marion Bell. There are ice caves under the north rim containing a miniature glacier.

Folsom, east of Johnson Mesa, is the site of the discovery of a stone spearpoint in the ribs of an extinct species of bison which established the existence of man around 10,000 years ago. From the vicinity of Folsom one can see the volcanic Emery Peak (7,350'). This peak and the gap west of it were named for Madison Emery, who settled in New Mexico in 1865. Somewhat farther north on State Road 325 is the wooded Devoy's Peak (6,740'), which was named for Michael Devoy who came to the state in 1870 and founded the first post office in the later Union County. From Folsom, drive 7 miles southwest on State Road 325 to Capulin National Monument.

Capulin Mountain (8,215'), 29 miles east of Raton and near U.S. 87, is a volcanic cindercone of almost perfect proportions. It is preserved as a National Monument, since 1916. The base of the mountain can be reached also from the village of Capulin on the south side. A three-mile spiral road leads from the base to a parking area at the rim. The rim is circled by a foot trail and has paths leading to the bottom of the crater 415' below. The mountain is named for the chokecherries (capulin) which grow on its slope. It consists of cinders, ash, and rock debris from volcanic explosions and is located in an area of former volcanic activity. The region has lava flows, squeeze ups, pressure ridges, vents and lava bombs. From the rim one can see other volcanoes including Laughlin Peak (8,836') and Sierra Grande (8,720') which is nearly 40 miles long at its base. On a clear day, Rabbit Ears Mountain (5,940') north of Clayton can be seen. This notched volcanic mountain is named for a Kiowa chief, Rabbit Ears, who is buried there. It was a landmark on the alternate Santa Fe Trail. Near the monument are remnants of the Santa Fe Trail and the famous Goodnight Trail over which some 250,-000 cattle passed on their way to Colorado, Wyoming, and Montana in the 1860s. The rim also offers excellent views over the distant Sangre de Cristo Mountains and the Spanish Peaks in Colorado.

The Taos Region

From Taos one can go into the high country below Wheeler Peak by driving north through Arroyo Seco and up the Rio Hondo (deep river) valley. Ski lodges are located 15 miles northeast at the former mining town of Twining, where accomodations can be had the year around.

A beautiful circle trip from Taos starts out on U.S. 64 east of there. The road goes up the Taos River (Rio Fernando de Taos) Valley and crosses Palo Flechado Pass (9,107'). This pass is near the old Taos Indian trail to the buffalo plains. At the summit of the mountain, there was a tree into which the Indians shot the arrows remaining after the buffalo hunts, which explains the name Palo Flechado (tree shot with arrows). On the east side of the pass the road drops into the peaceful Moreno (dark) Valley, with Eagle Nest Lake (8,135'). The 140' dam at the outlet of this lake was built by the Springer brothers in 1912.

State Road 38 north of Eagle Nest goes to the ghost mining town Elizabethtown, which was wide-open during the gold rush of 1868. At Red River Pass (9,852') north of Elizabethtown the road crosses the divide between Red River and Moreno Valleys. From the summit a large part of the Taos Range, including the Wheeler Peak area, is visible. On the west side of the pass the road goes through the resort town of Red River and continues down the beautiful Red River Canyon to Questa. State Highway

3 leads back to Taos from Questa through the foothills of the Taos Range.

Costilla Pass (9,700') between Moreno Valley north of Eagle Nest and the Costilla Creek drainage is on a dirt road on private property and may not be traveled without permission.

A side trip from Eagle Nest to Cimarron goes through the scenic Cimarron Canyon. Ute Park (7,706') in the upper canyon was a Ute village and later the terminus of the railroad to the gold mines in the Baldy region. The Cimarron Palisades in the lower canyon are sandstone cliffs which rise several hundred feet from the canyon floor. The town of Cimarron has buildings and ruins which are reminders of the gold rush, the days of Lucien Maxwell, the Utes, and the Indian Agency. Not far distant from Cimarron are the Philmont Boy Scout Ranch, Kit Carson's Rayado Ranch, and the boundary of the vast Vermejo (vermillion) Park, a private game preserve containing almost half a million acres of woodland and mountains.

The road from Questa to the Colorado State Line (State Road 3) goes through the old Spanish village of Costilla. West of the village is the wooded Ute Peak (10,151'), named for the Indians who once lived there. A secondary road east of Costilla leads to Amalia and beyond to the upper Costilla Creek (on private land). It is possible to continue by jeep to the Latir Lakes.

The Brazos Mountain Range

The mountain region between Tres Piedras (three rocks) and Tierra Amarilla (yellow earth) extending from El Rito to the Colorado border is in part in Carson National Forest and on the Tierra Amarilla Land Grant. It contains mountains which are grouped together as the Brazos Mountain Range, the spectacular Brazos Cliffs along the Rio Brazos, and three mountains with characteristic shapes, Jawbone Mountain (10,680') Tusas (10,150') and Brokeoff Mountain (10,365'). On the east side is the great volcanic dome of San Antonio Mountain (10,935'). Excellent highways (U.S. 84 and 285) parallel the area on the east and west, but the region itself is still primitive. A new road between Tres Piedras and Tierra Amarilla, which is to follow parts of the old stagecoach road, is only in the planning stage. A trip around the area starts at Hernandez, 6 miles north of Espanola. U.S. 84 goes northwest from there past the northern end of the Jemez Mountains through Abiquiu and Tierra Amarilla to Chama. From there State Road 17 goes to the Colorado border along the narrow gauge railroad, over Cumbres (10,022') and La Manga (10,230') Passes and through the Conejos Valley to Antonito, where it meets U.S. 285. The route south goes past the east side of San Antonio Mountain through Tres Piedras and Ojo Caliente (Spanish, hot water) back to Hernandez. San Antonio Mountain has a jeep road to the top which starts from U.S. 285 on the east side. A network of secondary roads leads to the lookout on Kiowa Mountain (Kiawa Peak) and campgrounds at Lagunitas, Canjilon Creek, El Rito, and El Ritito.

The Jemez Mountains

This area includes one of the most spectacular volcanic regions in the country which can be seen almost in its entirety from good roads. From Santa Fe drive north through the Miocene lake bed formations to Pojoaque, a former Indian Pueblo. Turn west on State Road 4 to Los Alamos, cross the Rio Grande at Otowi Bridge past mesas capped with lava flows, and climb through deeply eroded canyons of volcanic ash and tufa on South Mesa Road to the south side of Los Alamos Canyon (south of the bridge). From here continue south on West Mesa Road to the junction of State Road 4 at the Bandelier National Monument boundary. As an alternate route, one can drive past White Rock and Bandelier National Monument through the ponderosa forest to the same junction.

Route 4 climbs steeply over the rim of the Jemez caldera with magnificent views over the upper Frijoles (Spanish, beans) Creek and San Miguel Ridge with St. Peters Dome lookout to the distant Sandia Mountains near Albuquerque and then drops into the huge Valle Grande which is part of the Jemez caldera. An alternate route from here over Del Norte Pass (8,985') leads to the ghost mining town of Bland and the pueblo of Cochiti. This scenic route is open in the summer, but the pass is snowed in during the winter months. At the southern end of the Valle Grande the road goes around the southern base of Redondo Peak, past Jemez Falls into the steep Jemez River Canyon. Side trips from this part of the highway on secondary roads can be made to El Valle de los Indios, Cerro Pelado, and Sulphur Springs.

State Road 4 in Jemez Canyon goes by steep canyon walls with lava flows, past Soda Dam, Jemez Cave, Jemez Hot Springs, Jemez State Monument, the monastery Via Coeli, and Jemez Pueblo. Volcanic formations line the canyon for miles until farther down sedimentary rocks become prevalent again. At San Ysidro, State Road 44 is reached, which leads to Bernalillo, passing the pueblos of Zia and Santa Ana and the Coronado State Monument. The return trip to Santa Fe on U.S. 85 passes the northern end of the Sandia Mountains, the Cerrillos (hills), and the lava flows on top of Bajada Hill.

An alternate trip from the west side of the Jemez Mountains at La Cueva on State Road 126 traverses the Sierra Nacimiento near the old copper mines. The return trip from Cuba on State Road 96 goes around the San Pedro Mountains on the northern end of the Sierra Nacimiento. Side trips on secondary roads lead to San Gregorio Lake, the San Pedro Parks Wild Area, and Dead Man Peak. Near Coyote on State Road 96 the prominent Cerro Pedernal comes into view. Beyond Coyote the road crosses Abiquiu Dam and joins U.S. 84 to Espanola and Santa Fe.

The Southern Sangre da Cristo Range

Within recent years State Roads 3 and 75 have been paved and it is now possible to drive around this entire mountain area on all-weather roads. Starting in Santa Fe drive southeast on U.S. 84-85 along a part of the old Santa Fe Trail through Apache Canyon and over Glorieta Pass (7,432'). Side trips on secondary roads can be made from there to Glorieta Baldy lookout, to Pecos, and to Cowles on a scenic road along the Pecos River. U.S. 84-85 follows along the base of Glorieta Mesa, crosses the Pecos River and passes Starvation Peak before it turns northeast toward Las Vegas. Side trips from here to Montezuma and El Porvenir give magnificent views of the steep faces of Hermit Peak. From Las Vegas, State Road 3 goes north past Storrie Lake State Park to Mora. At Holman it climbs Holman Hill and drops beyond into the Rio Pueblo Valley. From there State Road 3 continues over U.S. Hill to Taos. State Road 75 follows the Rio Pueblo into the Peñasco Valley which borders on the Picuris Range on the north side and the Truchas Range on the south.

A new road from Peñasco goes past Picuris Pueblo (Pikuria, those who paint) and drops in gentle grades to Dixon and the Rio Grande Valley at Embudo (Spanish, funnel), where it reaches U.S. 64 which leads to Espanola and Santa Fe. An alternate trip from Peñasco through the old Spanish villages of Las Trampas, Truchas, and Chimayo to Espanola is well worthwhile, even though the road is not entirely paved.

From Santa Fe one can drive directly to Hyde Park and from there to the Santa Fe Ski Basin at an elevation of over 10,000'. A picnic ground and a coffee shop at the ski area are available.

Albuquerque Region

The skyline of Albuquerque is dominated by the rugged west face of the Sandia Mountains with their steep ridges, faces, and towers. These mountains are accessible by road from Tijeras Canyon. From the city limits drive east on U.S. 66 past the village of Tijeras, 8 miles to the junction of State Road 14. Turn north on this road and drive 7.5 miles to a fork at 8,652'. You will pass Sandia Peak Ski Area, which has restaurants, and a lift to the top of the ridge at 10,378'. Stay left on Sandia Crest Road and drive 12 miles through aspen woods to the Sandia Crest Observation Point (10,678'). The view of almost 100 miles in all directions includes many of the mountain ranges in New Mexico. To return, drive 4.3 miles to the junction with the loop drive, State Road 44, take the left fork that descends through Las Huertas (the gardens) Canyon and return to Albuquerque via Placitas and Bernalillo. Near Las Huertas picnic ground the road passes the trail to Sandia Cave where one of the most important archaeological discoveries in the state was made. The cave is now open to the public.

Two campgrounds and the start of a trail at the base of the western face of the Sandias can be reached by secondary roads from Juan Tabo Boulevard or from Alameda.

The Manzano Mountains south of Tijeras have a paved road along the entire east slope which connects Tijeras with Mountainair. The road goes through the Spanish villages of Escabosa, Chilili, Tajique, Torreon, and Manzano. Chilili, Tajique, and Torreon are built near the ruins of the Saline Pueblos which were abandoned in the 17th century because of Apache raids.

Cedro Peak in the northern Manzanita section can be visited as a side trip on a secondary road. It offers views over Tijeras Canyon and the southern part of the Sandia Mountains. Farther south the Tajique-Torreon Loop Road goes through Tajique Canyon which has fine stands of maple trees. Secondary roads from Manzano lead to Capilla Peak (9,375') and Red Canyon campground (7,500').

The Quarai Ruins State Monument preserving the ruins of the 17th century mission church is just off State Road 14 near Punta de Agua, 8 miles north of Mountainair. Another ruin of the same period (abandoned in 1670) is found in Abo State Monument, 9 miles west of Mountainair. The return trip goes over Abo Pass on U.S. 60 and north on U.S. 85 in view of the western face of the Manzano Mountains. The John F. Kennedy picnic area on the west side of the mountains can be reached by road from Belen.

The Sacramento Mountains

The large valley extending more than 100 miles north of El Paso, Texas, the Tularosa Basin, is bordered on the west side by the San Andres-Oscura Range and on the east by the Sacramento Mountain Ranges. It contains extensive lava flows and the gypsum deposits of the White Sands National Monument. The main north-south highway, U.S. 54, runs on the east side of the basin through Carrizozo and Alamogordo. Most of the west side including the San Andres and Oscura Mountains is now in the White Sands Missile Range.

In the vicinity of Corona, U.S. 54 goes through the foothills of the Gallinas Mountains. It continues south past the dome-shaped uplifts of the Jicarilla, Patos, and Carrizo Mountains on the east and the malpais on the west to Carrizozo. The lava flows, which came from Little Black Peak and Broken Back Crater, is accessible from the Valley of Fires State Park approximately 3 miles northwest of Carrizozo.

State Road 349, 4 miles north of Carrizozo, leads northeast to the ghost mining town of White Oaks at the foot of Carrizo Mountain; secondary roads from there continue to Jicarilla and Ancho.

U.S. 380 east of Carrizozo runs south of Carrizo and Tucson Mountains and crosses the Sacramento Range at Indian Divide (6,996'). On the eastern slope it continues along the south side of the Capitan Mountains. Secondary roads from Capitan and Hondo circle this range and a Forest Service road traverses these mountains at Capitan Gap (7,452'). Points of interest along U.S. 380 are Smokey the Bear's Museum, Fort Stanton, the Fort Stanton Caves, and Lincoln State Monument.

The mining village of Nogal can be visited by driving south from U.S. 380 on State Road 37, 6 miles west of Indian Divide. This road connects with State Road 48 at Angus. Continuing south on State Road 37, one comes to Alto and Ruidoso, resorts and gateways to the Sierra Blanca Mountains. Side roads lead up Bonito Creek, to the lookout Mon Jeau, and to the Sierra Blanca Ski Area. From Ruidoso one can return to the Tularosa Basin by way of U.S. 70 over Apache Summit and Mescalero, or continue south on the eastern slope on State Road 24 to Cloudcroft.

A more scenic road to Cloudcroft, however, is U.S. 83 which turns off from U.S. 54, 3 miles north of Alamogordo. The paved highway goes through the western scarp of the Sacramento Mountains with its steep valleys and cliffs of sandstone and the only highway tunnel in the state. Near the summit the road passes the old wooden trestle of a former railroad from Alamogordo to Cloudcroft.

Sunspot, the solar observatory of the U.S. Air Force, is 17 miles south of Cloudcroft on paved road. Regular tours of the observatory are scheduled once a week. A popular circle drive includes Sunspot, the road south from there along the Sacramento River, and the return along the rim of the Sacramento Mountains to High Rolls on State Road 83. Trips on the east slope of the mountains to Mayhill on State Roads 84 or 24, or the Forest Service road along the upper Peñasco Canyon, go past the scars of the Allen Canyon Fire which burned 16,700 acres of forest in 1951. Near Mayhill, Captain H. W. Stanton, for whom the fort is named, lost his life in a battle with Mescalero Apache Indians.

State Road 24 on the east slope of the Sacramento Mountains connects with roads in the Guadalupe Mountains, but they are more easily reached from U.S. 285. State Road 137, 12 miles north of Carlsbad, is paved to Sitting Bull Falls. Continuing on State Road 137 one can drive to the rim of the Guadalupes and along the rim to the north end of the range.

The Mogollon Volcanic Plateau

A large part of southwestern New Mexico is included in the volcanic plateau which extends west from the Black Range to the Arizona border, and from the Plains of San Augustin to the Deming Plain. Most of this area is accessible by paved roads.

From U.S. 85 south of Caballo, State Road 90 leads west through the mining towns of Hillsboro and Kingston and over the Black Range at Emory Pass (8,178′) to the Mimbres Valley.

State Road 27 from Hillsboro to Lake Valley was the old stage-coach road to the rich silver mines in the region.

In the Mimbres Valley one can drive south to the City of Rocks State Park or continue west to the vast Santa Rita open-pit copper mine and beyond to Silver City, from where all parts of the plateau can be reached. State Road 90 south from there to Lordsburg crosses the Big Burro Mountains and the continental divide south of Signal. Secondary roads lead to the old model mining town of Tyrone and to Leopold in the Burro Mountains mining district.

U.S. 180 north of Silver City passes through the western edge of the plateau. It crosses the continental divide just west of the city at 6,230′ and winds through Drunken Man Canyon to the Catron County line. Continuing north in the San Francisco River valley, the road goes through Glenwood and Alma and over the Saliz Mountains at Saliz Pass (6,436′). From the junction with State Road 12 north of the pass, U.S. 180 climbs northwest over the Frisco Divide to Luna and then into Arizona. State Road 12 goes northeast through Reserve, Apache Creek, and Aragon, crosses the Plains of San Augustin, and meets U.S. 60 at Datil, from where one can circle the area via Socorro and U.S. 85 on pavement.

Side roads from this main loop which are not entirely paved lead into the Gila National Forest and some of the more remote mountain country in this region. From Glenwood one can drive to the Catwalk in Whitewater Canyon.

A 235-mile circle drive around the Gila Wilderness Area starts at Alma, climbing in numerous curves to the ghost town of Mogollon on State Road 78 and then over the Mogollon Mountains at Silver Creek Divide into the Gila River drainage. The road continues past the Tularosa, Elk, and Long Canyon Mountain Ranges, O-Bar-O and Black Mountains, and the Beaverhead Ranger Station, to the Mimbres Valley, and returns to Silver City by way of Santa Rita and Fort Bayard.

The Inner Loop scenic drive goes from Silver City to Pinos Altos at the continental divide, then along Cherry Creek, across the Pinos Altos Mountains and into the Sapillo Creek drainage. Where the road crosses the creek, it forks, the left fork (State Road 15) continuing to the Gila Cliff Dwellings. The right fork (State Road 35) passes the new recreation area at Roberts Lake and Camp Thunderbird and returns by way of State Road 61 and the Mimbres Valley.

Still another drive circles a part of the Black Range from Truth or Consequences. Traversing the range at Emory Pass, one can drive north in the Mimbres Valley on State Road 90 to the Beaverhead Ranger Station, turn east on State Road 59, and recross the range a short distance east of Boiler Peak. State Road 52 on the east side leads back to U.S. 85 via Cuchillo. A short side trip brings one to the former mining town of Chloride.

In the northwest section of the area jeep roads traverse the Gallo Mountains at Jewett Gap and the Spur Lake Basin east of Jim Smith Peak (9,100').

Climbing and Hiking Trails

The mountains of New Mexico are crisscrossed by foot and horse trails extending hundreds of miles in all directions from towns, villages, and roads into the regions of higher altitude. Most of those in the National Forest are maintained by the Forest Service and are in good condition. Older trails which are not maintained are passable if one does not mind stepping over fallen logs.

In the following chapters the mountains in the state are grouped under mountain ranges, starting in the northern part of New Mexico. For completeness sake, those on private property and those with few or no trails are listed also. Mountains primarily visited for technical climbing are found in the chapter on rock climbing.

The shortest routes and trails are given together with alternate routes and any other information which is available. The accompanying trail maps show the mountain ridges in heavy black as divides between drainages, boundaries of National Forests, land grants, and Indian Reservations, rivers with their tributaries, roads and trails (maintained or not). Those using the trails are asked to respect private property and to obey the few posted rules of the Forest Service within the National Forest.

THE SANGRE DE CRISTO MOUNTAINS

The highest, largest, and most important mountains in New Mexico are in the Sangre de Cristo Range which forms the western boundary of the Great Plains. Its beginnings at the southern end lie in the foothills east of Santa Fe and west of Las Vegas. From there the ridges continue north for nearly 200 miles to the vicinity of Salida, Colorado.

From the Colorado state line to the region of Taos these mountains are folded into two main north-south ranges, the Taos Mountains on the west and the Cimarron Range on the east side, enclosing between them the picturesque upper Costilla and Moreno valleys. The lower mountains west and immediately south of Taos, the Fernando and Picuris Mountains, are remnants of old east-west ridges which interrupt the general north-south trend and permit the crossing of the mountains over relatively low passes. South and east of Peñasco the ridges run north and south again, forming the high Truchas and Santa Fe ranges on the west side and the Mora and Las Vegas ranges on the east.

The Precambrian core of the Sangre de Cristo Mountains is exposed at the higher elevations in the Taos Range, at the Truchas Peaks, and in the Santa Fe Range. Elsewhere the overlying sediments form the summit ridges, as in the Las Vegas Range. The deep gorges in the mountains frequently cut through the softer sandstones and limestones and expose the Precambrian formations beneath. Examples are found in the Pecos, Santa Barbara, and Red River drainages. Faults run mainly north and south along the entire distance between the Colorado state line and Santa Fe. The northern part of the range is complicated by vol-

canic action, and the regions of higher elevation, particularly
Truchas and Wheeler Peaks, have been further modified by glacial
action.

In old Spanish documents these mountains are often referred
to as "La Sierra," "La Sierra Madre," or "La Sierra Nevada."
According to legend the mountains north of Santa Fe were first
named Sangre de Cristo in the 17th century or, perhaps more pre-

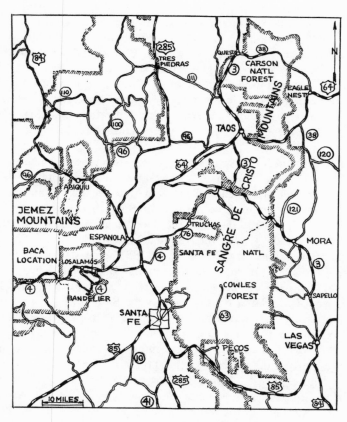

SANTA FE AND VICINITY

cisely, during the Pueblo Revolt of 1680. A dying padre Juan supposedly asked for a sign from heaven and exclaimed, "Sangre de Cristo," when the mountains turned red at sunset. The location of this event is not certain. It could have occurred at Santa Clara, Taos, or Tesuque Pueblos, for at each a padre Juan was martyred.

The Sangre de Cristo Mountains were the hunting grounds for Apache and Comanche Indians and the Spaniards ventured into them only in heavily armed groups. The first Spanish excursion into these mountains was De Vargas' expedition to capture the fleeing Picuris in 1696. Guided by a Taos Indian, he crossed the mountains east of Picuris Pueblo and overtook them some miles east of there. The return trip was started in a driving blizzard which caused the loss of 200 horses and 5 mules. The trip through immense snowdrifts by way of the Mora Valley to Pecos required 10 days. There is little indication that there were other extensive explorations of these mountains during Spanish times.

The demand for beaver pelts to make stovepipe hats caused the first thorough exploration of the western mountains by the trappers, who followed each little stream into the high country. In the Sangre de Cristo Mountains only Spanish trappers were allowed prior to 1820. Foreign intruders were arrested and their furs confiscated. Under the Republic of Mexico these barriers were removed, and between 1821 and 1823 some 100 trappers following Indian trails collected furs in the Pecos and Rio Grande valleys. By 1826 the beaver was nearly extinct in the area. The 1827 map of the Santa Fe Trail shows the Sangre de Cristo Range as "Impassable Mountains." The territorial maps are still quite similar but for the first time some of the peaks are named. In the maps of 1851 and 1855 the names of "Mora" and "Moro" peaks appear in the vicinity of the Truchas mountains.

A venture into the upper reaches of the Santa Fe River was described in 1844 by the Santa Fe trader Josiah Gregg. A more extended survey of this valley was made by Lt. Gilmer, Capt. Murphy, and Private Grooms from Fort Marcy in 1847, but evidently neither group got beyond the lake which is still some distance below Lake Peak.

In 1863 a remarkable man, Giovanni Maria de Augustino, arrived in Las Vegas after walking the Santa Fe Trail all the way from Council Grove, Kansas. He stayed in a cave at Romeroville, ministered to the poor and sick, and was regarded as a holy man. When his solitude was disturbed, he moved to a cave 250' below the rim of a mountain known locally as "Cerro del Tecolote" (owl peak), where he remained until 1868. The mountain was climbed frequently since 1863, and annual pilgrimages by the Sociedad del Eremitano are being continued to the present day. Since 1863 the mountain was called Mount Solitario in memory of the hermit and, later, "Hermit Peak."

Gold was found in the Moreno Valley in 1866. Thousands of men swarmed into the valley in 1867, and the adjacent mountains were prospected. The first recorded ascents of the major peaks, however, must be credited to the surveyors of Lt. Wheeler, whose parties climbed Truchas, Wheeler Peak, Lake Peak, and Santa Fe Baldy during the years 1873-75. They prepared an excellent map and described the climate, geology, mineral resources, and vegetation of the Sangre de Cristo Mountains.

Gold discoveries at Twining and Red River in 1880 caused extensive prospecting in these valleys, but the more important molybdenum ore was not discovered until 1910. The Pecos Mine at Terrero produced zinc and lead ores from 1916 until they were exhausted in 1939. The ore was hauled from Terrero to Pecos by an aerial tramway that left a scar in the hills, visible to this day. Other mining ventures near Rociada, Mineral Hill, Cordova, and Picuris have remained small operations, some of which are still continuing at the present time.

The most important event in the Sangre de Cristo Mountains near the turn of the century was the establishment of the National Forests. During the 19th century the forests were regarded as inexhaustible and there was little concern when 12 million acres burned in 1891, Far sighted men like Gifford Pinchot supported legislation authorizing forest reserves. Such legislation was passed

in 1891, and in 1892 the Pecos River Forest Reserve in the Sangre de Cristo Mountains, the second oldest national forest in the
United States, was created by proclamation of President Harrison.
Legislation to regulate the forest reserves was passed in 1897.
The Division of Forestry was transferred to the Department of
Interior in 1905, renamed the Forest Service, and the reserves
were called National Forests. When Carson National Forest was
created in 1906, the greater part of the Sangre de Cristo Mountains went under the Forest Service administration's multiple use
program which protects the watersheds but permits regulated
grazing, timber cutting, and recreational activities. The fastest
growing use is recreation, which includes mountaineering and all
its aspects.

The Taos Range

The northernmost section of the Taos range, north of Costilla
Creek, is a continuation of the Culebra Range in Colorado. The
bare ridge has a broad summit which is known locally as Big
Costilla Peak (13,005'). This peak is on private property. The
top of the ridge forms the boundary between the Sangre de Cristo
Grant and Vermejo Park. Permission is required to enter and
inquiries should be made in Costilla.

The part of the Taos Range between Costilla Creek and Red
River can be reached from Questa. It appears on Taos and Vicinity quad, and on the map of Carson National Forest in which most
of the range is located. To get to this area drive 24 miles north
from Taos on Highway 3. Near the junction of the Red River
Highway (State Road 38) turn northeast on a marked gravel road
and drive 7 miles along Cabresto (Spanish, rope) creek to a fork.
The left road goes to Cabresto Lake (9,200'). The last part of
the road is quite steep and rocky and should be driven with
caution.

Cabresto Peak (12,462'). From Cabresto Lake campground
(9,500') ascend the ridge north of Cabresto Lake 2 miles to an

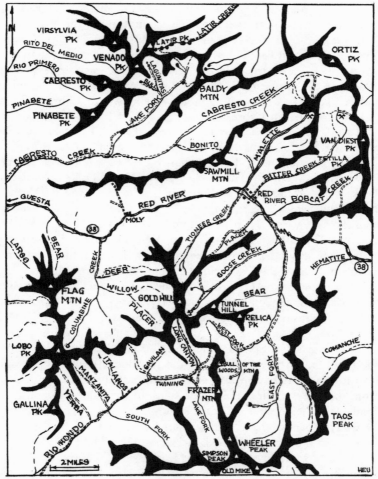

unnamed peak (12,039′), continue west 0.5 mile, cross the divide, and climb 0.5 mile northwest to the summit.

Pinabete (Spanish, fir) **Peak** (11,953′) and **Venado** (Spanish, deer) **Peak** (12,447′). Using the same approach as for Cabresto Peak, hike southwest on the divide 2 miles to Pinabete Peak, or northeast 1 mile to Venado Peak. A much longer trail running along the divide over the Pinabete summit joins the main road near the National Forest boundary, 2 miles northeast of Questa. Venado Peak can be climbed also from Bull Canyon or Lagunitas Creek. For the return trip one can drop due east from Venado Peak into the cirque using the southwest couloir to the Lagunitas Lakes (11,600′), follow Lagunitas fork down to Cabresto Lake fork, and return to Cabresto Lake.

Latir Peak (12,723′) and **Virsylvia Peak** (12,600′) can be climbed from Cabresto Lake by the same approach as Cabresto Peak, from Lagunitas Fork, from Bull Creek, or from Heart Lake, which lies farther north on Lake Fork, at 11,400′. Virsylvia Peak is the prominent bald mountain 1 mile northwest of Venado Peak, from which it can be climbed. The 1958 Army topographic map shows a Virsylvia Peak north of Latir Peak. This is probably an error. To climb Latir Peak from Venado Peak it is necessary to traverse around the rocky ridge at the head of the Lagunitas cirque and climb the Latir ridge 1 mile northeast of there.

The Latir Lakes (also called Nine Lakes) and the north side of Latir Peak are on private property (Sangre de Cristo Land Grant). For northern approaches to these lakes drive 19 miles north from Questa on State Road 3 to Costilla and from there 6 miles southeast on State Road 196 to Amalia. Continue 11 miles southeast on a primitive road to the junction of Latir Creek and jeep to the third Latir Lake, staying right at the sawmill. A trail from the upper Latir Lakes leads south to the ridge which can be climbed to the summit of Latir Peak.

Baldy Mountain (12,043′). From Cabresto Lake hike 5 miles along Lake Fork to the Forest Service cabin. The trail above the cabin leads to Baldy Mountain (1 mile) and continues beyond along the entire ridge to the Midnight Mine. From the ridge near Baldy Mountain one can look down on the north side into the Baldy Blue Lake which is on the Sangre de Cristo Grant.

The mountains which lie on the ridge between Cabresto Creek and Red River and at the head of the Cabresto and Bitter Creek valleys are usually climbed from the Red River side.

Sawmill Mountain (10,936′). Drive up Malette Creek 1.5 miles above Red River to a big meadow. There is a trail in the canyon on the left (north) side which can be followed for 1 mile. Then climb west 1 mile directly to the peak. The trail continues on the west side in Bonito Canyon and runs into the road on the south side of Cabresto Creek.

Van Diest Peak (11,222′), **Tetilla Peak** (10,800′), and **Ortiz Peak** (11,185′) are wooded summits on the east side of the Taos Range. They are accessible from Malette Canyon. The jeep road in this canyon leads from Red River to the Midnight Mine. From there hike east 1 mile to the Anchor Mine. Climb east to the ridge on the old stagecoach road and follow the ridge 1.5 miles south to Van Diest Peak and 1 mile beyond to Tetilla Peak. Ortiz Peak is 2.5 miles north on the ridge above the Anchor Mine.

The prominent mountain ridge east of Highway 3 between Arroyo Hondo and Questa has three named summits: Flag Mountain near Questa, Lobo Peak in the center, and Gallina Peak at the south end.

Flag Mountain (11,938′) and **Lobo** (Spanish, wolf) **Peak** (12,106′) can be climbed from San Cristobal, which is located on a well-marked side road a few miles north of Arroyo Hondo. Cars may be parked along a primitive road which starts up San Cristobal Creek. From the end of this road hike 5.5 miles on the trail along the creek to the top of the ridge. To climb Flag Mountain go north on the ridge 1.5 miles to the summit. There is a trail for the first mile to the head of Lama Canyon.

Lobo Peak is 2 miles south on the ridge from the same saddle. The rocky ridge still has remains of an old trail on it. A better approach to Lobo Peak is from the Rio Hondo road to the Taos Ski Valley. Trails in Yerba (4 miles) and Manzanita (4.4 miles) Canyons lead almost directly to the peak. The latter is the better trail. Both connect also with the Forest Service trail from Gold Hill to San Cristobal.

Gallina Peak (10,893′) can be reached by going south on the ridge from Lobo Peak. There is no trail. The distance is 3 miles.

Wheeler Peak (Taos Peak) (13,160′), the highest mountain in

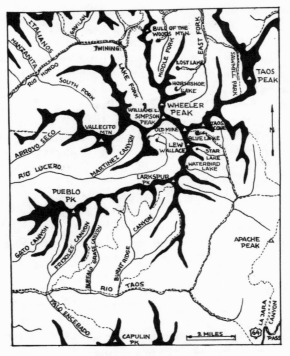

WHEELER PEAK REGION

New Mexico, is on the Taos and Vicinity quad. It can be climbed from Rio Hondo, the Red River Valley, or from Eagle Nest. For southern approaches drive 3 miles north from Taos on Highway 3 to the junction of State Road 150. Drive north on this road through the village of Arroyo Seco and continue up the Rio Hondo valley 15 miles on the old toll road of the Wm. Frazer Company to Twining (9,412′), a former copper-mining town. Campgrounds are available all along this road and at Twining, which is the location of several ski lodges with ample accomodations. Wheeler Peak is accessible from Twining by two routes.

For the shortest approach hike 4 miles southeast to Williams Lake (11,000′). It is possible to jeep the first 2.5 miles. Climb

2 miles east from the lake to the summit. A longer route (8.5 miles) utilizes the mine road to Bull of the Woods Mountain (11,610′) which turns off from the Williams Lake road. The top of this mountain was at one time mined for low grade copper ore and the jeep road is still passable in good weather. From Bull of the Woods continue south 4.4 miles on the ridge trail to the peak which now lies within the Wheeler Peak Wild Area. The ridge around Williams Lake offers much better climbing. It can be followed from the ski area to Wheeler Peak and beyond to Bull of the Woods Mountain, a trip which has been accomplished in one day.

The Red River Valley has a modern paved road from Questa to beyond the town of Red River. Two miles southeast of Red River a gravel road goes up the east fork to the location of the old ditch cabin at 9,868′ northeast of Wheeler Peak. Although there were cabins at regular intervals along the ditch, only one such cabin site appears on the maps.

Follow the ditch trail 1.5 miles south, take the first fork marked "Lost Lake" to the right, and climb 1.5 miles south and west to this lake at 11,300′. The ridge west of this lake can be climbed by choosing a route through the bowl in which the lake is located. Wheeler Peak is 2 miles south on the ridge. The descent can be made by the same route or by dropping from the ridge to Horseshoe Lake. A dim trail near the creek leads back to the East Fork. A somewhat longer route from Red River Valley by way of the Middle Fork and Middle Fork Lake goes over Bull of the Woods Mountain. There is also a new modern trail from the Middle Fork jeep road to Lost Lake (distance, 3.4 miles).

To approach Wheeler Peak from Eagle Nest, drive west on the road to Idlewild and beyond to the first locked gate. Continue on foot or horse approximately 3 miles to Sawmill Park, where the trail to Taos Cone, Old Mike, and Wheeler Peak will be found.

A much longer trail to the Wheeler Peak region starts from Highway 64 at the last sharp curve in La Jara Canyon, west of

Palo Flechado Pass (9,107'). One can drive 2 miles north into La Jara Canyon. From there the trail leads over Apache Peak (10,164') north along the ridge to Taos Cone (12,277'), Old Mike (13,135'), and Bear Lake, avoiding the Indian Special Use Area. The distance from the highway to Apache Peak is 6 miles and to the Wheeler Peak Wild Area, 16 miles.

Frazer Mountain (12,150') is a small prominence on the Wheeler Peak ridge, 2 miles north of the peak. It is reached from the Blue Lake Trail by a 150 yard side trip west of the trail. Continuing south on the trail, the next high point is Mount Walter (named after the Santa Fe photographer, H. D. Walter).

Simpson Peak (12,850') is the small bare mountain 0.4 mile south of Wheeler Peak, over which the Blue Lake Trail goes. It is located at the junction of the ridges and is misplaced on the Taos and Vicinity quad.

Old Mike (13,135') is the prominent bare peak 2 miles southeast of Wheeler Peak at the head of the Blue Lake Valley. Both Simpson Peak and Old Mike can be climbed easily from Wheeler Peak. They are also accessible directly from Williams Lake by going south to the low point in the cirque at 12,400' and climbing northeast to the ridge trail. A longer descent route through Lucero Canyon has been used.

Gold Hill (Golden Hill) (12,682') is north of Twining and is usually climbed from there. Take the Bull of the Woods road one mile northeast to Long Canyon and hike 5 miles north on the trail in this canyon to the summit. The mountain can be climbed also from Goose Lake on the east side, which is reached from the east fork of Red River by a 12-mile jeep road along Placer Creek and over the ridge into the Goose Lake drainage.

Vallecito Mountain (12,600') at the head of the Rio Hondo South Fork is easiest to reach from Williams Lake. The distance is about 3 miles and the loss in altitude from the cirque is 900'. The mountain is on Indian land and permission may be required to climb it.

The Blue Lake Trail runs from Red River over Gold Hill, Bull of the Woods Mountain, Frazer Mountain, Wheeler Peak,

Simpson Peak, Old Mike, and Larkspur Peak. It enters the Taos Indian Special Use Area south of Old Mike. This area is sacred to the Indians and closed to the public. A limited number of permits has been issued in past years to enter the area. Such permits are issued by the Taos District of Carson National Forest and countersigned by the War Chief of Taos. During 1964 the Taos Indians refused to sign any permits. Within the Special Use Area are located Lew Wallace Peak (12,438'), Larkspur Peak (12,000'), and Pueblo Peak (12,282'), Blue Lake, Star Lake, and Waterbird Lake. Holders of permits may hike from Taos Pueblo on a trail going east along the Rio Taos. It branches after 2 miles, where the Simpson Memorial trail turns off to the left (northeast). The Burnt Ridge trail turns off to the north 3 miles farther upstream and the trails meet just south of Larkspur Peak. The Blue Lake trail runs close to the top of Larkspur Peak and continues north to Old Mike. Lew Wallace Peak is a short distance east of the trail. There are no maintained trails to Pueblo Peak.

Tunnel Hill (11,670') and **Relica Peak** (11,784') in the upper Red River drainage can be climbed from the West Fork. A pickup can be driven 2 miles up this canyon. Then climb 1.5 miles northwest to the saddle west of Tunnel Hill and east 0.5 mile to the summit. Relica Peak is 1.5 miles southeast on the ridge from Tunnel Hill. The loss in altitude between the peaks is 400'. One can descend the same way or return by way of Bear Canyon or Goose Creek.

Taos Peak (11,220') is usually climbed from Sawmill Park, which is 3 miles southeast by jeep from the ditch cabin site. Hike 1 mile east to the top of this peak.

The southern end of the Taos Mountains is a low wooded east-west ridge between the two forks of the Rio Taos (Rio Pueblo de Taos and Rio Fernando de Taos). A Forest Service trail runs over the entire length of this ridge. It starts just east of Cañon on State Road 64 (east of Taos) inside the forest boundary and runs northeast 2 miles to **Devisadero Peak** (8,300'), an Indian fire lookout, continues 5 miles northeast and east to

Capulin Peak (10,104′), and 3 miles farther east to **Casita Piedra Peak** (10,453′). The trail continues in part on an old logging road until it reaches State Road 64 after 5 miles.

The low east-west ridge south of Highway 64 is called the Fernando Mountains. The old South Boundary Trail of Carson National Forest runs near the top of this ridge. Starting from Cañon the trail leads southeast from Highway 64 to **Cerrito Colorado** (10,235′) (distance 5 miles), continues southeast over the **Sierra del Don Fernando** (10,363′) and branches near Osha Mountain. The north fork leads to State Road 38 near Black Lake, and the south fork crosses the Rincon Mountains and eventually comes out at Tres Ritos on State Road 3.

The Cimarron Range, a narrow north-south range forming the eastern boundary of the wide Moreno Valley, continues north to the vicinity of the Colorado state line. Both the mountains and the river which originates there are named for the bighorn sheep (carnero cimarron), once native to the region.

The Cimarron Range is entirely on private land. It was originally a part of the Sangre de Cristo Grant, given to the fur traders, Beaubien and Miranda, by Governor Armijo in 1841. Both were killed in the Taos Revolt of 1847 and the grant eventually came into the possession of Lucien Maxwell, who had married one of the Beaubien daughters. Maxwell settled on the grant near Rayado, establishing a trading post, and took up ranching. U. S. surveyors determined in 1850 that his grant contained 1,714,000 acres.

Ute and Jicarilla Apache, who considered the grant lands their ancestral hunting grounds, continued to hunt in the mountains and a band of Utes lived in Cimarron Canyon near the present Ute Park. They traded with Maxwell, occasionally bringing gold nuggets.

While trading at Fort Union in 1866, an Indian showed two soldiers a pretty rock which was recognized as copper ore. The soldiers, Kroenig and Moore, paid the Indians to show them the source at the top of Baldy Mountain, the later location of the Mystic Lode. Three other men, sent into the Cimarron Mountains to assess the value of the find, discovered gold in the sands of Willow Creek where they camped. Hordes of men swarmed into the Moreno Valley in the following year, 1867, when they heard the news, and in 1868 an estimated 7,000 people were crowding the valley. In the same year, Elizabethtown was organized 5 miles north of Eagle Nest and soon could boast of 7 saloons, 5 stores, 1 drug store, 2 hotels, and 3 dancehalls. Gold was found in every gulch around Eagle Nest. The chief mining districts were in Willow and Ute Creeks, others in Michigan Gulch, Grouse Gulch (The Spanish Bar), and Humbug Gulch. One of the richest mines, the Aztec in Ute Creek Valley, produced over 3 million dollars' worth of ore. The original site on top of Baldy Mountain was named "Mystic Lode" when gold was found there.

Lack of water soon led to the building of the "Big Ditch," a 42-mile canal from the Red River Valley with aqueducts, one over a valley 79' deep. The ditch cost $280,000 and was completed in 1869. It led the dammed-up waters of Middle Fork, Lost, and Horseshoe Lakes to the East Fork and from there to Red River Pass and Humbug Gulch. Mining activities declined in the 1870s. A 5-mile tunnel which was built from the Deep Tunnel Mine (10,500') on the west side came out at the Aztec Mine. Some gold and molybdenum were found, but the tunnel never paid expenses. A dredge named Eleanor, which was used in the lowlands in 1901, finally disappeared in the silt opposite Elizabethtown. The railroad came to Ute Park in 1908 and was later extended to Baldy on the east side of the mountain. A revival of mining in the area in 1915, particularly at the Aztec Mine, exhausted the gold. The Deep Tunnel and Baldy Mines were operated until 1939. Maxwell tolerated these activities on his land when he received royalties, although in many cases these were only token payments. His investments in the mines brought small returns, and he sold the grant for an estimated $700,000.

The Ute Indians resisted the invasion of their lands by the miners as long as they could. They were subdued by troops stationed at Cimarron. An Indian Agency was maintained there for a time, but finally the Utes were removed to a reservation in southern Colorado. The source of their gold was traced to ancient diggings uncovered in the Aztec and Baldy mines.

The vast Maxwell land grant was resold and divided. One large section in the vicinity of Cimarron became the Philmont Boy Scout Ranch. Another, the 600,000-acre Vermejo spread, was sold in 1900 to W. H. Bartlett; in 1927 it was resold to a private club, and again sold in 1952. It is now maintained as a private hunting preserve.

There are 5 summits in the Cimarron Mountains which have been described in the early surveys. Hayden mentioned a Costilla Peak which was visible from Ponil Canyon. This peak was a triangulation station for the Wheeler surveyors, and its location was given as southeast of Costilla and on the ridge between the Costilla and Vermejo drainages. The mountain is now known as Little Costilla Peak (12,580′). It is on Vermejo Park property and accessible only by special permission. Little Baldy, somewhat farther south on the same ridge, is also on the Vermejo Ranch.

U.S. Geological Survey personnel have climbed and surveyed Baldy Mountain (formerly called Elizabeth Peak), Touch-me-not Mountain, and the smaller Hart Peak (Stony Point), 7,978′, on the east side near the Ponil Base Camp of the Philmont Ranch. Baldy Mountain and Touch-me-not Mountain, and the ridge joining them, form the eastern skyline of Moreno Valley. They are located on Ute Park quad and have been climbed from Eagle Nest. A few smaller summits in this range are south of Cimarron Creek and can be found on Tooth of Time quad.

Baldy Mountain (12,441′) and **Touch-me-not Mountain** (12,-045′) are the north and south summits of the main ridge northeast of Eagle Nest. The normal route to these mountains is the old mine road through the now abandoned settlement of Virginia City (8,900′) east of Iron Mountain and northeast of Eagle Nest (8,220′). Local inquiry should be made about permission and the way to the road which goes up Willow Creek. Jeep or hike this road as far as it appears passable and climb east to a low saddle (11,100′). There is no regular trail. Baldy Mountain is 1.8 miles north of the saddle. Climb northeast and north along the west side

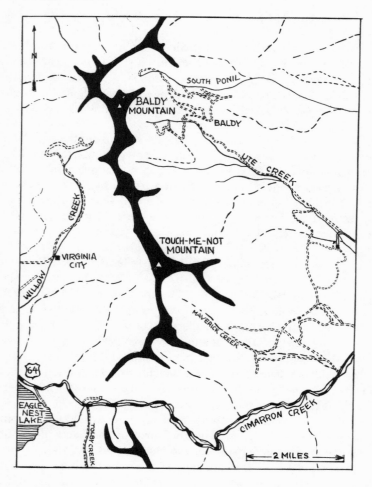

of the ridge to a high grassy saddle and then north to the summit, or climb from the mine road on scree slopes directly to the summit. Touch-me-not Mountain is on the same ridge 2 miles south-southeast from the low saddle. It derives its name from the reluctance of the former owners to grant permission to enter the mountain area. Approaches from the east side along Ute Creek are longer.

Summits on the Philmont Scout Ranch property south of Cimarron Creek include Comanche Peak (11,326'), Cimarroncito Peak (10,468'), Bear Mountain (10,663'), Black Mountain (10,892'), Bonito Peak (10,616'), Shaefers Peak (9,400'), Tooth of Time (9,003'), Grizzly Tooth (9,005'), Trail Peak (10,242'), Burn Peak (9,938'), Lookout Peak (9,922'), Crater Peak (9,748'), and Rayado Peak (9,805'). The mountains in this wooded area are accessible by trails. Arrangements for climbing on ranch property should be made at ranch headquarters.

The Picuris Range. The small Picuris Range on the east side of the Rio Grande Valley between Taos and Espanola is an east-west spur of the Sangre de Cristo Mountains. The ancient ridge is composed largely of Precambrian rocks. It has one broad summit, Picuris Peak (10,810'), which has a Forest Service fire lookout on its top. To reach the peak drive 2 miles east from Peñasco on State Road 75 to Vadito. On the east side of this village take a gravel road north to the peak. The road approaches the north side of the mountain, goes around the peak to the south side, and from there to the top, a total distance of 7 miles. The summit offers good views of the Taos and Peñasco Valleys and a large part of the Sangre de Cristo Mountains from Taos to Truchas.

The Southern Sangre de Cristo Mountains. The southern section of the Sangre de Cristo Mountains rises almost 7,000 feet, from the Vegas Grandes on the east side and the ancient Miocene lake bed on the west, and extends over a distance of 40 miles from Peñasco to south of Pecos. The 1827 map of the Santa Fe Trail shows the region as impassable mountains, and the trail swung wide around them. There are no roads across the high country, and some of the major summits are preserved much as they were 50 or 100 years ago in the Pecos Wilderness Area. The mountains on the west side form the Santa Fe Range. Near the Truchas Peaks an east-west ridge connects with the Las Vegas Range, forming a continuous mountain chain which encloses the upper Pecos Valley. This large wooded area is in Santa Fe

National Forest (one of the oldest in the country) and in the
Pecos Wilderness. The Santa Barbara drainage on the north
side is in Carson National Forest. While the region has been long
known for hunting and fishing, mountaineering is comparatively
recent even though there are 30 named summits and some are
accessible the year around. The early explorations were made
from the Pecos valley or from the Las Vegas side and mostly on
horseback. Only in the last 25 years have more people climbed the
peaks on foot from the shorter approaches from the west side on
new roads and trails.

The Truchas Region

The highest mountains in the area are the Truchas (Spanish,
trout) Peaks which are visible from the Espanola valley, the Pajarito Plateau (Los Alamos), and various points in the Jemez
Mountains. They are perhaps the most popular mountains in the
region, partly because they are more precipitous than other parts
of the range.

When seen from a distance, either from the Pecos valley or
from the Rio Grande, three Truchas Peaks can be distinguished.
The highest summit, South Truchas, is easily identified because
it stands somewhat apart on the southern extremity of the group
and has a smaller peak on its south ridge, Little South Truchas.
The other peaks are more difficult to recognize, but if one looks
at the mountains from South Truchas or from any of the ridges
joining them, it becomes apparent that there are actually four summits. North Truchas forms the divide between the Rio Quemado
and the Santa Barbara West Fork. One peak is on the ridge in
the middle between North and South Truchas and another on a
spur which runs west from there. The former is the prominent
peak visible from the Pecos River basin which has a light vertical
streak of quartzite running through the summit. This is the
Middle Truchas referred to by Elliot Barker, the late Santa Fe
photographer H. D. Walter, and others who have approached the
mountains from the southeast. According to U.S.G.S. data, how-

ever, this peak has never been surveyed, although it is higher than
North Truchas and has a prominent location in the center of the
group. The survey sheet for Middle Truchas refers to the "sharp
prominent peak" which is visible from the west, and is located
in a northwesterly direction from the south summit.   There is

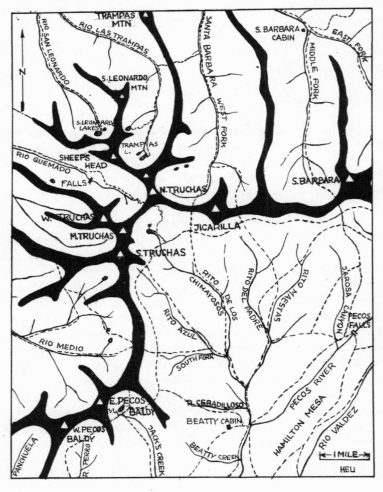

little doubt that this a different peak on the west side of the cirque and that there are therefore two Middle Truchas Peaks. Sutherland and Montgomery in *Trail Guide to the Upper Pecos* refer to the peaks as East and West Middle Truchas. Other names have been introduced, but it appears most appropriate if the name "Middle Truchas" is retained for the east summit, and if "West Middle Truchas" is shortened to "West Truchas."

The first recorded ascent of the Truchas peaks was made by the Wheeler survey party, who established survey stations on the south summit and mapped the region in 1874. Their map of 1877 is a beautiful piece of work which compares favorably with the most recent maps and gives an elevation of 13,150′ for "Las Truchas" peak. The topographic survey of the watershed was let out later under contract to a private firm and was carried out in 1888-89. The first topographic map based on this survey was issued in 1894, and reprinted as late as 1948 without change. It contained a number of errors and listed a mountain half a mile north-northwest of North Truchas with an elevation of 13,306′. For almost 60 years this peak was regarded as the highest point in New Mexico. The error was found by H. D. Walter of Santa Fe in 1948 when he checked the altitudes of the summits with an altimeter and found that the highest Truchas peak was lower than Wheeler Peak. Subsequent measurements by the U.S.G.S. engineer G. W. Forney have confirmed these findings and established an altitude of 13,110′ for South Truchas. More precise measurements in 1952-54 have furnished a set of reliable elevations for the major peaks in the region, but topographic quadrangle maps are available only for a small section on the west side. South Truchas (13,102′) is the highest summit in the area, followed by West (Middle) Truchas (13,066′), and North Truchas (13,024′). Middle (East) Truchas is estimated to be near 13,070′ high. The altitudes of Jicarilla (12,944′) and Santa Barbara (12,641′) represent older measurements and are probably less accurate, but East (12,529′) and West Pecos Baldy (12,500′) have been surveyed more recently. The altitude of Trampas Mountain is given as 12,175′, and the peak north-northwest of North Truchas (Sheepshead), once regarded as the highest point in New Mexico, is estimated at only about 12,600' in altitude.

The shortest approach to the Truchas Peaks is from the village of Truchas on State Road 76. From the village drive east on a gravel road 8.5 miles to the start of the Truchas irrigation ditch, which was built in 1850. Jeep one mile beyond to the junction of the ditch with the Rio Quemado or hike on the path along the ditch. Find the trail on the north side above the river and follow the river 6 miles upstream, keeping north around the Quemado Falls. The headwall at the source of the Rio Quemado is known as the "Amphitheater," a magnificent cirque flanked by three Truchas Peaks and two additional summits. North Truchas on the east side of the cirque drops off in a large step toward an unnamed peak with steep east face which represents the junction of the Truchas and Trampas mountain ridges. Another summit towers on the north side over the Quemado Falls. This is called Sheepshead from its appearance from West Truchas Peak. The mountains bordering the Pecos Valley have been drawn up for this book in a series of six overlapping area maps. New quadrangle maps are also available.

South Truchas or Las Truchas (13,102') can be climbed in 2-3 hours from the Truchas amphitheater (11,500') by going up any one of the scree slopes to the top of the ridge, continuing to the summit of Middle Truchas (13,070'), and following the ridge south 0.5 mile to the top. There is a trail to the top of the ridge on the south side of North Truchas, but the scree slope on the southeast side of the amphitheater is faster. The summit has a small rock shelter, a cairn, and remnants of the survey marker. For many years there was a small shrine to the Virgin Mary mounted on a pole. It disappeared in the stormy winter season about ten years ago.

North Truchas (13,024') is reached from the amphitheater in 2 hours. Find the switchback trail on the east side of the amphitheater to the lowest part of the ridge. Climb ¼ mile northeast on the ridge to the summit. Return the same way or by the north side. An alternate somewhat longer route uses the Forest Service trail to the Trampas Lakes. From the village of El Valle, drive southeast to the end of the road at the junction of the Trampas and San Leonardo Rivers, pack 7 miles along the Rio Trampas to the Trampas Lakes. The trail starts on the north side of the river. From the lakes climb southwest 0.5 mile to the low point of the ridge and follow the ridge 1 mile southeast to the summit. A still longer route from the west fork of the Santa Barbara River is seldom used.

West Truchas (13,066′) can be climbed from the amphitheater either by the two large couloirs which run on the sides of the east face, or by the northeast ridge. Choose a route from the amphitheater to the top of the northeast ridge and follow the ridge ¼ mile to the summit. The east face was first climbed by a Los Alamos mountaineer party led by Tom Stephenson on September 30, 1955. This is a roped climb, and there is loose rock hazard in the upper part of the route. Take the south couloir half-way up. Then work north to the couloir which runs to the center of the peak, climb out on a shelf on the north side and head straight for the summit.

Sheepshead (12,600′) can be climbed readily from the San Leonardo Lakes. The lakes are 6 miles from the junction of the Trampas and San Leonardo Rivers. The Forest Service trail follows the river upstream. Climb the large couloir south of the lakes to the saddle and from there to the top of the ridge. Continue south ¼ mile to the summit. The entire ridge can be climbed to its northern end. It offers good views of the Trampas Valley and the third Trampas Lake which is known as "Laguna Escondida" (Hidden Lake). The summit on the northern end of the ridge is San Leonardo Mountain (12,400′). For rapid descents from this mountain, the avalanche gully in the north face goes. Continue in the dry creek beds to the Trampas River trail.

The entire amphitheater ridge can be climbed in one day by a strong party. Climb Sheepshead from the amphitheater, San Leonardo, or Trampas Lakes and follow the ridge to North Truchas. Continue on the slow ridge to Middle Truchas and the West Peak and descend to the amphitheater by the northeast ridge.

Approaches from the Pecos Valley are uniformly longer and start either from Pecos Baldy Lake or the Lone Tree (Truchas) Lakes.

Jicarilla (Cerro Chimayoso: Spanish, the mountain of the Chimayo people) (12,944'). From Peñasco on State Road 75, drive south on State Road 73 to Rodarte, turn left at 1.5 miles and continue 5.5 miles to the Santa Barbara campground which has prepared campsites. Only conditioned parties can expect to make the 28-mile round trip in one day. From the campground take the well-marked trail south along the Santa Barbara River.

The trail crosses to the east side of the river and the west fork trail branches off where the valley begins to widen. Take this trail and camp in the timber below the ridge on the west side of Jicarilla, if desired. Climb to the summit from the saddle. Return the same way, or find the dim trail down from the east saddle which rejoins the main trail below the peak.

Santa Barabara, or Santa Barbara Baldy (12,641'). From Santa Barbara campground hike the main trail south 6 miles to the trail junction near the Santa Barbara Cabin. Continue upstream 6 miles via the middle fork, or 7 miles via the east fork. From the ridge hike up to the summit. Experienced groups have made the round trip in one day. There are sites suitable for camping in the timber below either saddle. Santa Barbara can be climbed also from the Pecos side, from Tres Ritos, from the Rio de la Casa west of Cleveland, or from Le Doux southwest of Mora.

Jicarita (Spanish, little basket) (12,750'). This mountain was named Jicarilla on the Wheeler Survey map. From Santa Barbara campground hike the main trail 6 miles south to the trail junction of the east fork and find the trail which switchbacks 3.5 miles east to the top of the ridge. Follow the ridge north 1 mile to the summit. An alternate route from Tres Ritos is longer. From Angostura campground on the west side of the Rio Pueblo, take the Serpent Lake trail 12 miles to the ridge and climb 1 mile north to the summit. For a faster descent to Santa Barbara campground

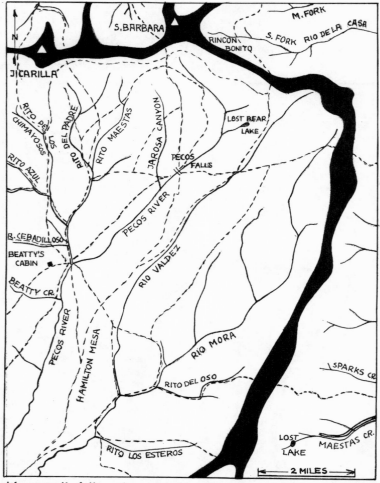

without trail, follow the west ridge from the summit over an old burn.

East Pecos Baldy, formerly called Cone Peak or The Cone (12,529′) has been climbed from the Santa Fe Ski Basin, from Truchas, and from Cowles. It is accessible from the west by the

Rio Medio trail. Drive southeast on the rough road which fords the Rio Quemado just west of Cordova to the start of the Rio Medio trail. Hike 6 miles to the Brazos Cabin and continue east 5 miles to the ridge and south 1.5 miles to the summit. From Cowles (8,200′) take the Panchuela or Round Mountain trails

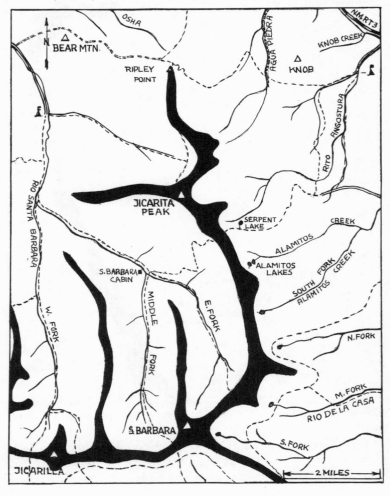

10 miles to Pecos Baldy Lake (11,742′). A good trail on the south side of the lake leads 0.5 mile west to the summit. Pecos Baldy Lake can be used for camping.

West Pecos Baldy (12,500′) is reached by a 1-mile ridge walk from the east summit. It is also accessible by the west ridge from

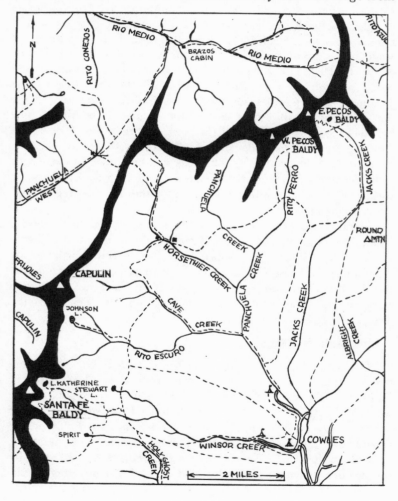

Horsethief Meadows and from Capulin Peak. The top of the west ridge is slow because of fallen timber.

Trampas Mountain (12,175′). This summit is a prominent peak visible from the west side near Truchas village and from the Jemez Plateau and is recognizable by large rock slides in the form of a figure "S." To reach the mountain drive from Truchas 9 miles northwest to Las Trampas (Spanish, the trap) and 1 mile beyond to a road fork. Take the right fork 3 miles to El Valle and continue on the new Forest Service road past the ruins of the El Diamante Ranch to the junction of the Trampas and San Leonardo Rivers. Take the trail on the east side of the Trampas River 4 miles southeast to a trail junction and follow the switchback trail 1 mile east to the saddle of the ridge. The trail between the Santa Barbara west fork and the Rio de las Trampas crosses the ridge about 60 feet northwest of the low point in the wooded saddle. The peak can be climbed by a longer route from the Santa Barbara campground by way of the west fork. The mountain offers fine views of the Truchas region and the river valleys.

Sierra Mosca (Fly Mountain) (11,801′), a prominent wooded mountain southwest of South Truchas Peak, is on the Sierra Mosca quad. It can be climbed by a 2-mile trail northwest of the Panchuela West Cabin which in turn is accessible from the Rio Medio or the Rio Frijoles valleys from Cordova or Cundiyo respectively. The summit affords magnificent views of the Truchas Peaks.

The Santa Fe Range

The summits in this range can be seen from U.S. 84-85 between Santa Fe and Las Vegas and from U.S. 64-84 north of Santa Fe. There are a number of spectacular bare spots on the west side of these mountains, two on Lake Peak with outlines of a horse's head and a sheep, and one on Santa Fe Baldy which resembles a thunderbird. They represent remnants of disastrous fires of the past. In Spanish times the Indians hunted deer by setting fire to mountain sides and fires frequently raged unchecked in the region, until the National Forests were established. One of the first of these was the Pecos River Forest Reserve, established in 1892. The largest recorded fire started in the Big Tesuque Canyon in May 1887. Its origin is uncertain but, although it was discovered soon, no attempt was made to fight it. After several days it had burned the slopes of Lake Peak, Santa Fe Baldy, and Pecos Baldy, creating the bare slopes which are still visible, crossed north of Cowles and burned across the Las Vegas Range to northwest of Wagon Mound, where it was finally checked more than two months later by a crew cutting railroad ties. The fire barely rated a newspaper mention and the Department of Interior, which was notified, did not deem it important enough to fight the fire for an estimated $600.

Once hunting ground and sacred territory of the Pueblos, the peaks in the Santa Fe Range were climbed and surveyed by the Wheeler survey party in 1873-75. The region was opened to the public when the Hyde Park road was extended to the Aspen Basin over the protests of the Indians. The eastern approaches by way of Holy Ghost Canyon and Windsor Creek are trails.

Lake Peak (12,409') appears on Aspen Basin quad. Since the establishment of the Santa Fe Ski Basin, the road to the foot of the peak is kept open the year around and the climb has become a favorite both in summer and winter. The well-marked road from Santa Fe takes about an hour to the ski basin (10,564'). In the summer an alternate route is available from Tesuque. The basin has ample parking facilities, a picnic ground, a coffee shop, and a lift with bucket seats to a bare summit (11,182') near the top of the Horse's Head. A poma lift to the summit of Tesuque Peak (12,047') was added in 1963. From the ski basin climb 1.5 miles east to the top of the ridge, either from the top of the tow over the burn, or through the woods east of the lodge. Follow the ridge 1 mile north to the summit. Santa Fe Lake (11,600') is visible east of the ridge. The lake, Santa Fe Canyon, and McClure Reservoir are part of the Santa Fe water supply and are closed to the public. The last part of the ridge is bare granite and in the winter rope and ice axe are recommended. West face routes from

Nambe Lake should be used with caution because of loose rock hazard. A short climb ¼ mile east from the peak by trail leads to Penitente Peak (12,249'). One can return the same way or make a 5-mile circle trip by way of Nambe saddle and the Win-

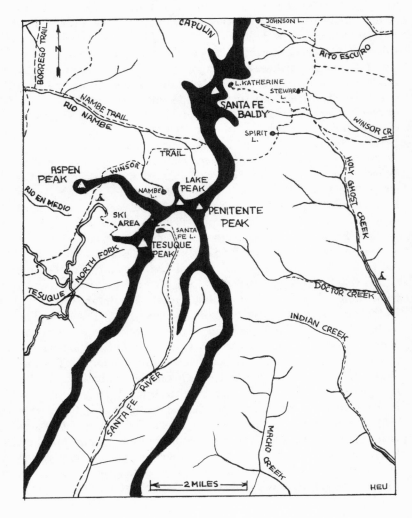

sor trail. Lake Peak can be climbed also from Nambe Lake (11,400′) by way of the Winsor trail.

Santa Fe Baldy (12,622′), also known as Old Baldy or Baldy Peak, appears on Aspen Basin quad. From the Santa Fe Ski Basin picnic ground find the Winsor trail on the north side below Aspen Peak. This trail runs 4.5 miles to the Nambe saddle, From the junction of the Nambe and Winsor trails just below the saddle climb north 1 mile to the summit. The mountain has been climbed from Cowles by hiking from the Winsor Creek campground 8 miles west to Lake Katherine (11,742′) and climbing 0.5 mile west on a large scree slope to the summit. Lake Katherine, a beautiful fishing lake, which is stocked from the air, can be reached also from Nambe Saddle by a trail which now skirts the mountains on the east side. The lake is named for the late Katherine Cavanaugh who visited it often from the Los Pinos Ranch near Cowles.

Capulin Peak (12,200′) lies 2 miles north on the ridge from Santa Fe Baldy. Strong parties can do both mountains in one day. The peak may be climbed also by the somewhat longer route from Horsethief Meadows along its northeast ridge.

Glorieta Baldy (10,199′) and **Thompson Peak** (10,554′) are on the McClure Reservoir quad. Although the former can be climbed by a 5-mile trail from the Glorieta Baptist Assembly, the top can be reached by a jeep road to the fire lookout. Drive 2 miles east from Glorieta on the old Pecos Road, turn north on the gravel road to the lookout and jeep 12 miles to the summit. For Thompson Peak, find a trail on the east side of the Glorieta Baldy summit knoll which follows the ridge north 2 miles to the peak. Fallen timber just south of the summit can be avoided by staying on the west side below the ridge.

The Las Vegas Range

Most of this mountain chain lies sufficiently far back from the roads so that it is not easily identified. Only the sheer faces of Hermit Peak, which stands apart from the main ridge, are evident

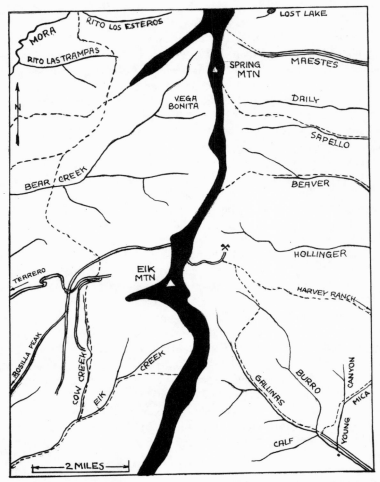

from all sides. A fork of the Santa Fe Trail went over the southern end of the ridge near Barillas Peak. General Kearny marched
from Las Vegas through Kearny's Gap and then essentially along
the present road to Pecos and from there to Santa Fe. The mountain region was first explored from the east side by pioneers like

George Beatty and Professor Dyche and became known to other visitors to the Harvey Ranch, and later the Montezuma Hotel of the Santa Fe Railroad.

Elk Mountain (11,661'), also named Rincon on older maps, is the bare-topped summit visible from the Santa Fe Range as the high point of the ridge on the east side of the Pecos valley. To reach the mountain from Pecos, drive 14 miles north on State Road 63 to Terrero. Near the site of the American Metals Mine on the north side of Willow Creek, take the jeep road or hike 10 miles east to the top of the ridge. The summit is ¼ mile south. The road was used during World War II as access to the mica mine on the east slope of the mountain above Burro Basin. The first road leading south, 8 miles east of State Road 63, goes to Rosilla Peak (10,500') fire lookout. From the Las Vegas side the only route to Elk Mountain at present is through private property. Permission should be obtained at the Terrell Ranch in Evergreen Valley, 23 miles west of Montezuma. Follow the trail west of the ranch along the Gallinas River to Burro Basin and from there west to the top of the ridge. The distance is 7 miles.

Spring Mountain (11,500') is named after the little spring just below its crest. It can be climbed from Sapello Creek but the shortest route is the 4-mile ridge trail from Elk Mountain.

Hermit Peak (El Solitario, El Cerro del Tecolote) (10,060'). This prominent peak with its precipitous faces can be seen from Highway 85, both east and west of Las Vegas. It resembles a face lying horizontally and pointed to the sky, particularly when seen from west of town. It is easily accessible from West Las Vegas. Drive 5 miles north to Montezuma, the site of the former hotel of the Santa Fe Railroad, then follow the Gallinas Valley 8 miles upstream past Gallinas village to the junction of the Porvenir road. Turn north and drive 3 miles to the end of the road at El Porvenir Lodge (private). The 5-mile trail to the summit starts just east of El Porvenir and goes up the deep gorge which bisects the mountain. The east, south, and west sides of Hermit Peak are nearly vertical granite faces which have perhaps not been climbed. The deep canyon of Hollinger Creek lies between Hermit

Peak and El Cielo (10,000') on the west side (Porvenir Canyon). Granite cliffs line this canyon for several miles. A steep tower on the west side at the entrance of the canyon is still unclimbed. Caution is indicated on all routes other than the standard trails. There was one fatality on the peak in 1953. The trail going up Hollinger Creek (Porvenir Canyon) starts on the south side of the bridge just below El Porvenir Lodge, continues up the creek to the junction of Beaver Creek, and along this creek to the divide between Elk and Spring Mountains.

Starvation Peak (7,042'), a well-known landmark, on Villanueva quad, just south of Highway 85 near Bernal, is a flat-topped mesa which according to legend got its name because a party of colonists was starved out on its summit by Indians. Artifacts found on top indicate that it was used as a lookout by Indians long ago. In recent years there was an airplane beacon on its summit, regularly serviced by a lady caretaker who took the steep trail on the south side to the summit. The peak is easily climbed by this trail. The beacon was removed in 1964.

Barillas Peak (9,300'), the Forest Service fire lookout on the south side of the Las Vegas Range, is visible from Highway 84-85 between Las Vegas and Santa Fe. The old access road from San Geronimo (the Big Cross trail) is no longer usable. The peak can be reached from Pecos by a new road through Lower Colonias. The distance is approximately 20 miles.

Ridge Trails. The bare ridges of the southern Sangre de Cristo mountains offer fast and easy routes through the wilderness and beautiful views of the area. A continuous trail runs from Barillas Peak to Jicarita and beyond. The ridge from Jicarita to Pecos Baldy by way of the Truchas Peaks is passable and continues south from there around Horsethief Meadows to Lake Peak. Parts of these ridges were used by the author to hike from Cowles to Tres Ritos (1949), from Truchas over the West and South Truchas Peaks to Cowles (1956), and from the Santa Fe Ski Basin to Cowles by way of Santa Fe Baldy, Capulin Peak, and the Pecos Baldy Ridge (1955). In view of the long distances of such trips, they should be attempted only by experienced mountaineers. Other trails such as the old Borrego (sheep) trail from Truchas to Santa Fe are still maintained.

THE JEMEZ MOUNTAINS

The prominent group of mountains northwest of Santa Fe on the west side of the Espanola Valley extends from Cerro Pedernal, west of Abiquiu, to Borrego Mesa, near Jemez Pueblo. The central feature of the range is a large circular volcanic bowl, nearly 15 miles in diameter, which appears as early as 1779 on a Spanish map of Nuevo Mexico as "Valle de los Bacas." Once regarded as the world's largest volcano, the Valle Grande and its sister valleys, Valle San Antonio, Valle Toledo, Valle Jaramillo, and the Valle de los Posos, are now believed to represent a caldera, a basin formed by the collapse of the surface in the vicinity of volcanic activity.

The more recent volcanic eruptions from the caldera in the early Pleistocene period some 5 million years ago created the Pajarito Plateau by deposits of incandescent ashes, 1,000' thick over an area of 400 square miles. The present steep canyons and mesas were carved out of the tableland by the erosive forces of water and wind. Forest has gradually grown over the region except for the meadows in the ancient lake bed at the bottom of the valles and a few bare slopes on the mountains. The major summits are on the high eastern rim and in the southwest corner of the caldera, where there is also one of the more recent craters, El Cajete. Volcanic formations, however, extend for miles in all directions, and there are hot mineral springs at Sulphur Springs and in the Valle San Antonio in the caldera.

The region has been inhabited since ancient times. The finding of a fluted point on the plateau may signify occupation by man as early as 10,000 years ago. Most of the archaeological findings

Lake Katherine. *Photo by Author.*

Truchas Mountains. *Photo by Author.*

Hermit Peak. *Photo by E. C. Anderson.*

Santa Fe Baldy. *Photo by Author.*

West Truchas Peak. *Photo by Author.*

Shiprock. *Photo by E. C. Anderson.*

Lake Peak. *Photo by Author.*

Brazos Cliffs. *Photo by E. C. Anderson*

point to a large population during the Pueblo period from 1250 to 1500 A.D. Numerous ruins, caves, and petroglyphs remain as evidence. Some of the best are preserved in Bandelier National Monument. Others, such as the Puye Ruins, are on Indian land, still others are in the National Forest.

At least two pueblos claim ruins on the Pajarito Plateau as their ancestral homes. Ancient trails crisscross the area, and shrines on mesas and summits have been used by the Indians within recent times. Shrines on Pelado, the Tewa mountain of the west; Tschicoma, the center of all; and Redondo have been described and were intact as late as 50 years ago, but now there is almost no trace of them. The Jemez Mountains were visited since prehistoric times as a source of obsidian and chalcedony. Their steep cliffs and soft volcanic rocks offered building materials and locations for hideouts safe from marauding nomadic tribes. The fertile soil of the canyons permitted the raising of crops, and the woods were full of game. The decline of the population can be attributed to drought, nomadic Indians, and finally to the invading Spaniards. The surviving Pueblo Indians retreated to locations nearer water, where they are now living, and the Jemez mountains remained their hunting grounds until recent times.

Two of the early Spanish explorers visited the Jemez Sulphur Springs. Coronado's Captain Francisco Barrio-Nuevo took sulphur from there to Kuaua in 1540-42, and Oñate wrote in 1598 about the mountains of brimstone. A small sulphur plant was operated at the springs by Mariano Otero from 1901 until 1904. The most extensive mining in the Jemez mountains took place at Bland, south of the Valle Grande, where gold was found in 1889. The mines yielded over 2 million dollars in gold and silver

The caldera region of the Jemez range is completely within the Baca Location No. 1, which went to the Baca family in 1850 as compensation for its land holdings in the Las Vegas area. Much of the surrounding territory became Santa Fe National Forest, from which the Atomic Energy Commission received a portion for the establishment of Los Alamos. The Baca Location changed hands in 1880 and again at the turn of the century, when it was purchased by the Redondo Development Company, for which the mountain west of the Valle Grande is named. It was sold again in 1915 and in 1963 but has remained private grazing land, although proposals to make it a National Park were made as early as 1911 and are still under consideration.

The Jemez Mountains were climbed by the Wheeler survey parties during the 1873-75 survey. Santa Clara Peak (Tschicoma) was listed as a primary triangulation station, and its altitude was recorded as 11,507′, somewhat lower than later values. The summits in the region can be climbed easily, some of them having trails to the tops. More difficult climbing can be found in the steep-walled canyons, such as White Rock and Alamo Canyons, and on the cliffs west of Los Alamos, which have been used for practice climbing for several years.

Camping is permitted in Bandelier National Monument, in Santa Clara Canyon, and in the Santa Fe National Forest campgrounds. Various National Forest campgrounds are located on the south and west sides of the caldera region.

Tschicoma, or Santa Clara Peak, (11,561′) is the highest summit in the Jemez range. It is called Tsikomo by the Tewa and had a shrine on its top, which was regarded as the center of the Pueblo world. The most likely interpretation of the Indian name is "the place of much rock." The summit is located in Santa Fe National Forest and can be found on Polvadera Peak quad. The access road is on the Santa Clara Indian reservation and a fee is charged to enter the canyon and to camp. From Santa Clara on State Road 30 drive 20 miles west into Santa Clara canyon to the Kah-Po Recreation Area. Near the high point of the road at Tsikomo Pond a trail goes north 4 miles to the summit of Tschicoma; the last mile of the trail-less route goes over the large triangular meadow which is visible from the east side.

The ancestral home of the Santa Clara Indians is on Puye Mesa, where ceremonial dances are held each year in the summer. To get to the ruins, drive 4 miles south from Espanola on State Road 30 and west 7 miles to Puye (tree ring date 1527-62 A.D.). The road continues past Puye into Santa Clara canyon.

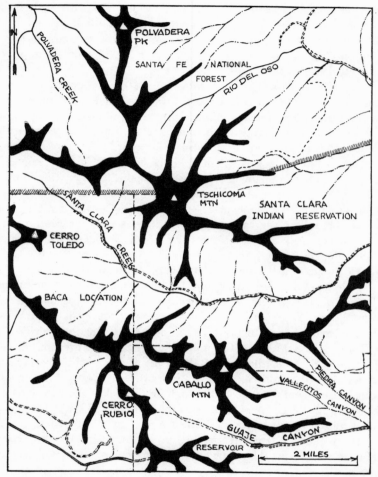

Polvadera (Spanish, dusty) **Peak** (11,232'), also called Abiquiu Peak, can be climbed from Tschicoma. Hike northwest and then north on the ridge between the peaks on a dim trail. The distance is 4 miles and the drop in elevation, 1,140'.

Cerro Rubio (Red Mountain) (10,449') on Valle Toledo quad can be climbed easiest from the south side. Take the trail from the low saddle in the pipeline road northwest to the junction of the Guaje canyon trail and climb 1 mile northwest on the ridge without trail to the bare rocky summit. The distance is approximately 1 mile.

Caballo (Spanish, horse) **Mountain** (10,496') on Guaje quad can be climbed from Santa Clara canyon. Drive 19.5 miles west from Santa Clara Pueblo, climb south to the top of the ridge, and follow it west and south to the summit. An easier route from the south side starts from Guaje (Spanish, gourd) Reservoir. From Barranca Mesa at Los Alamos, drive east on Escape Route 3 down Rendija (Spanish, crevice) Canyon to the junction of Guaje Canyon, or west on Escape Route 3 from State Road 4 below Totavi to the same place. Jeep Guaje Canyon west to the reservoir, follow the canyon on foot 2 miles past the reservoir to the marked trail, and climb the ridge north 2 miles to the summit. According to legend, Jesse James buried some treasure in Santa Clara Canyon on the slopes of Caballo Mountain.

Pajarito (Spanish, little bird) **Mountain** (10,441') on Valle Toledo quad is accessible summer and winter from the Los Alamos Ski Area. From Los Alamos drive south 1.7 miles on West Jemez Road to the junction of the Camp May Road and drive 4.5 miles to Camp May. A 0.5 mile hike west of the area on an old jeep road leads to the rim of the Valle Grande with spectacular views over the caldera. Find a trail near the crest of the ridge which leads south 1 mile to the highest summit. One can descend east and northeast by way of the other summit (10,300') and the ski trails, or south through Valle Canyon to West Jemez Road. In the winter the road from the Los Alamos Ski Area to Camp May is closed, but the picnic area can be reached by skis or snowshoes.

Cerro Grande (Spanish, Big Mountain) (10,199') on Frijoles quad and on the Baca Location is the first summit south of Pajarito Mountain. It can be climbed from there by dropping into the Valle Canyon saddle and climbing the summit ridge, a distance of 1.5 miles. The loss in altitude is 1,000'. The preferred route starts from State Road 4 near the Dome Road turnoff at 9,000', where the wooded south ridge meets the road. Old logging roads on the east side of this ridge lead north to a grassy saddle. The bare summit is north of there, total distance 1.5 miles.

Cerro Pelado (Spanish, Bare Mountain) (10,112') on Jemez Springs quad is the highest peak in the southeast corner of the Jemez caldera. The route to the mountain starts from State Road 4, 23 miles west of Los Alamos. Drive 5 miles south on State Road 290 to a rough primitive road turning north and marked: "Cerro Pelado Lookout, 7 miles." The road is suitable for jeep or pickup. The other summit of the twin peak is Los Griegos (9,933') and there is a spring in the saddle between them. Pelado was called Black Stone Mountain by the Indians, probably because obsidian is found there. Remains of a shrine on the summit are no longer visible.

Redondo (Spanish, round) **Peak** (11,254') on Jemez Springs quad was earlier known as La Sierra de la Bola (Mountain of the Knob). A shrine on its top was still visited by Pueblo Indians as late as 1911. The peak is located in the southwest corner of the Baca Location and is entirely on private land. Permission must be obtained to enter the property. The peak can be climbed from ranch headquarters in Valle Grande, in part on an old road going west. The distance is 2 miles. Alternate routes from the Sulphur Springs road on the west side or from where the south ridge meets Route 4 are much longer.

A few smaller summits on the south side of the caldera are accessible by trail. To climb **Rabbit Mountain** (9,938') on Bland quad, turn south in Valle Grande on the road to Cochiti. Near Del Norte Pass on this road take a logging road east 0.5 mile and hike 0.5 mile north to the summit. **Ruiz Peak** (9,208') and **Bear Springs Peak** (8,195') on Jemez quad, directly south of Cerro Pelado, are climbed from the Bear Springs road. Hike 4 miles northeast up Hondo Canyon in the National Forest. From the top of the canyon climb 0.5 mile northwest and $\frac{1}{4}$ mile west to the summit of Ruiz Peak. From the same road farther south at Bear Springs Forest Service Cabin one can climb **Bear Springs**

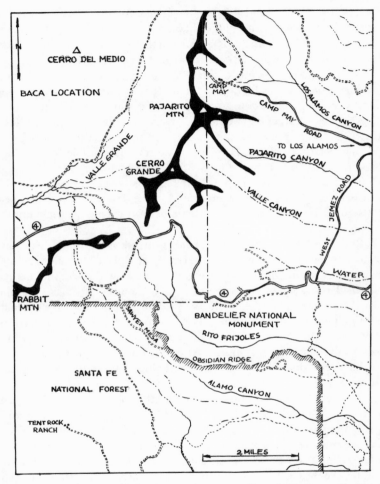

Peak. A 1-mile trail leads to the summit. A former lookout, **Bearhead Peak** (8,711′) on Cañada quad, can be climbed by a well-marked trail (9 miles) from Bland, on the Cochiti road. Peralta Canyon is accessible from the Bear Springs road. One can drive about 2 miles north into the canyon. From there an

11-mile trail leads to the Las Conchas Ranger Cabin. The canyon narrows 1.5 miles northwest of the end of the road until the cliffs are quite close. This section is called the Bear Jump.

Jemez Springs (6,000′), southwest of the caldera is the site of the Jemez State Monument which includes the ruin of one of the oldest missions, built in 1617 and destroyed in 1680, and the remains of Guisewa (pueblo of the hot place), one of the old homes of the Jemez Indians. On the west side of the steep-walled canyon behind the monastery of Via Coeli a jeep road and trail go to the top of Virgin Mesa, 1,800′ above the valley floor. Another pueblo of the Jemez called Amoxiumqua (ant hill place, tree ring date 1504 A.D.) was located on this mesa. The ruins are about ¼ mile from the rim. Other ruins on the east mesa are reached from Guisewa by an old trail which leads up the canyon past the spring. The healing waters of Jemez Springs have been used by Indians, Spanish, and modern man.

San Miguel Ridge. This mountain ridge on the southeast side of the Valle Grande is mainly in Santa Fe National Forest (on the Bandelier National Monument quad) and has trails leading to Bandelier National Monument. The high point of the ridge, St. Peters Dome (8,463′) can be reached by a secondary road from near the high point where State Road 4 crosses the rim of the caldera.

Boundary Peak (8,182′) is east of St. Peters Dome and can be climbed by its west ridge from the lookout road. The St. Peters Dome trail leads to the saddle from the last sharp curve in the road.

Obsidian Ridge (8,500′), one of the major sources of obsidian in the region, is located west of Bandelier National Monument Headquarters on the narrow ridge where Frijoles Creek and Alamo Canyon come closest together. It forms the boundary between Bandelier and Santa Fe National Forest. The 8-mile hike starts near the junction of State Road 4 and West Jemez Road south of Los Alamos. Take the first gravel road east of the junction on State Road 4, drive south a short distance, and park cars at the Bandelier boundary fence. Hike 1.7 miles to the Upper

Crossing and continue south on the opposite side of Frijoles Canyon 1 mile to the junction of Alamo Springs trail. Hike west 5 miles on Mesa del Rito to the narrowest part, using trails and old logging roads. Obsidian occurs at this point in layers of tufa (volcanic ash). One can return the same way or descend to the creek on the Frijoles side, avoiding the cliffs, and follow the trail back to the Upper Crossing. Rounded boulders of obsidian are found along the slope almost to the bottom of the canyon. Note: It is not permitted to remove obsidian. The old road on top of the ridge is closed to vehicular traffic but it is possible to hike down Sawyer Mesa from the Dome Lookout road 3 miles southeast to Obsidian Ridge.

An alternate approach to this ridge is from Route 4 west of the intersection with West Jemez Road. A dirt road 1 mile west of the intersection turns off south (left). It goes over a wooden bridge and continues 3 miles to the Apache Springs parking area. A trail from there leads 1.5 miles to the bottom of the canyon. Hike downstream a short distance to climb the ridge.

Cerro Pedernal (Spanish, flint mountain) (9,862′) is the flat-topped butte on the northern end of the Jemez range which has served since ancient times as a source of chalcedony (agate) for arrowheads, scrapers, knives, and spearpoints. It is located in Santa Fe National Forest and appears on Youngsville quad. The peak is reached from Abiquiu Dam, 2 miles west of Highway 84 and 7 miles north of Abiquiu. From the dam drive west on State Road 96, 10 miles to Youngsville and drive south 5 miles on the Encino Lookout Road to a meadow at about 8,000′, where cars may be parked. Chalcedony occurs near there at the base of the peak. Climb 3 miles east and northeast through the woods to the base of the summit ridge. There is an obvious break in the cliff on the west side of the peak to the left of a dark cave and near the north side of the mountain. A short scramble leads to a switchback trail which goes to the top on the north side of the quartermile basalt summit ridge. The east side of the mountain has been climbed but is considerably more difficult and is not recommended. Pedernal is said to have served as a refuge for

Indians in the past. Old Spanish mine shafts have been found in the vicinity, for instance, Las Minas de Pedro in the Arroyo del Cobre.

Southeast of Pedernal on Pueblo Mesa, south of Cañones, on Cañones quad, are the ruins of Tsiping which belong to the Pueblo Period, tree ring dates 1303-24 A.D. Visitors to the ruins are reminded that it is unlawful to disturb them or to pick up artifacts.

Two mesas on the east side of the Rio Grande are included in this section because they are of volcanic origin like the remainder of the Jemez Mountains and contemporaneous with parts of the Pajarito Plateau on the opposite side of the river.

Tunyo (Tewa, very spotted) (6,084′), the basalt-capped butte north of San Ildefonso Pueblo, is a famous landmark, popularly known as Black Mesa. This name is incorrect and misleading because there is a Black Mesa north of San Juan Pueblo. Tunyo served as a refuge for the Indians against the Spaniards who were unable to storm the steep sides. The old Spanish name, Mesa Huerfano, has not been used for some time. The mesa is found on Espanola quad.

According to legend the caves on the north side of Tunyo are the home of the giant Tsabiyo (or Savayo) who eats children. Pueblo mothers are said to make their children behave by threatening them with the giant.

Tunyo is sacred to the San Ildefonso Indians but permission to climb the mesa may be obtained from the governor of the Pueblo. A trail on the south side leads to the top. The summit has a fire shrine and ruins which are said to be remnants of pit houses.

Buckmann Mesa (6,547′) is the mesa directly south of Otowi Bridge on State Road 4 west of San Ildefonso, on White Rock quad. It can be approached from the old narrow gauge railroad bed on the east side of the river. Leave cars near the bridge and hike a short distance south on this road bed. Climb 300′ southeast along a scree slope through an obvious break in the rim rock to the top of the mesa (La Mesita, 6,300′) and continue directly to

the summit. The flat 1.5-mile long mesa east and below the summit cone has remains of the old Roybal homestead on it. Part of
this area is on Indian land and part of it is private property.
Traces of an old road to the ranch from Buckmann, a former
station on the narrow gauge, are still visible. South and east approaches were somewhat shorter when the Buckmann road from
Route 4 was still open but it is on Indian land and is closed at
present.

Clara Peak (8,549'), a Forest Service lookout, is accessible by
a jeep road (F.S. 144) which turns off west from U.S. 84, 1.5
miles north of Espanola. Drive west 8.5 miles to a junction and
north 5 miles to the peak. Continuing 6.5 miles west and north
beyond the junction one comes to the start of the Highline trail
which runs west to Cuba. This former horse trail crosses the
divide just north of Tschicoma Mountain and continues on a high
ridge which forms the divide between the Jemez and Chama river
drainages all the way to the San Pedro Parks Wild Area. The
service road F.S. 144 continues to Abiquiu. From Vallecitos on
this road a side road leads to the Cerro Pelon (9,367') radar site,
which is 15 miles from Abiquiu. From Vallecitos one can also hike
up Vallecitos Creek to the main ridge and from there to Polvadera
Peak, but this route is much longer than the route from Tschicoma.

SIERRA NACIMIENTO

This low north-south mountain ridge parallels State Road 44 from west of San Ysidro to beyond Cuba. It is a 50-mile long anticline with a granite core, flanked on the east by Paleozoic sediments. On the southern tip of these mountains there are extensive deposits of tufa and travertine around extinct spring craters, notably in the Arroyo Peñasco area. The Ojo del Spiritu Santo 4 miles northwest of San Ysidro is 20′ deep and 40′ in diameter and had hot water about 35 years ago. Some of the nearby springs are dry, others are filled with water. The area southeast of Cuba on the west slope of the mountains was mined from 1881 to 1960 and produced copper and silver valued over one million dollars. Most of the range is covered with ponderosa pine.

The southern section of the range has one small summit, **Pajarito Peak** (9,042′), on San Ysidro quad. This peak can be approached from the east side. Permission from the Pueblo Governor is required to drive on the road from Jemez Pueblo through Tecolote Canyon. This road goes within 0.5 mile of the summit. The Sierra Nacimiento is crossed by State Road 126 connecting Cuba with Jemez Springs and Los Alamos. The mountains north of this road contain the San Pedro Parks Wild Area, **San Pedro Peaks** (10,577′), and **Nacimiento Peak** (9,761′). All of this region is on Cuba quad and in Santa Fe National Forest. The San Pedro Parks area is essentially a high plateau of 10,200′ with several small peaks on the east side and one isolated summit on the south side (Nacimiento Peak). According to local legend, the Spaniards mined gold in the San Pedro Parks area. Trails within the area are accessible by roads from Cuba and Coyote.

The shortest route to **San Pedro Peaks** (10,577') follows the dirt road which turns south from State Road 96, 3 miles west of Coyote. Drive this road 8 miles southwest and 1.5 miles west to a trail which leads into the Wild Area. The mountain is 5 miles west and 1 mile north. For recent changes in the network of trails inquire at the Coyote Ranger Station. A trail on the southeast side of the Wild Area (No. 32) runs east on the northern boundary of the Baca Location and continues past Tschicoma Peak in the Jemez Range to the Santa Clara Peak road on the east side of the Jemez Mountains. The Rio Puerco, which flows from the northwest side of San Pedro Parks into Coyote Creek, has three waterfalls in the vicinity of the Rio Puerco campground. Also in the San Pedro Parks Wild Area 6 miles south of Gallina, on the wall of Gallina Canyon at 9,160', is Gallina Cave which was explored and surveyed in 1958, 1961, and 1962 by Explorer Post 20 of Los Alamos.

The wooded **Nacimiento Peak** (9,761') can be reached by trail from Gregorio Lake east of Cuba. A dirt road north of State Road 126 leads 3.5 miles to the lake past Nacimiento campground (9,000') and the peak is west of the lake. Trails from Gregorio Lake also go to San Pedro Peaks, 8 miles north.

Angels Peak (6,988'), on Bloomfield quad, is located approximately 70 miles northwest of Cuba and east of State Road 44. It is the chief landmark in the Garden of Angels, an 80 square mile area of badlands, and made up of blue and gray shale. The Angel Peak Recreation Site has picnic benches and shelters.

THE CHUSKA MOUNTAINS

The Chuska (or Choiskai—corruption of Shashgai, Navajo, white spruce) Mountains extend from Tohatchi north of Gallup to the Red Rock Valley in Arizona. The Tunitcha and Lukachukai Mountains in Arizona are usually included as subranges. The entire mountain range is on the Navajo Indian Reservation and the Chuska Plateau (particularly Chuska Peak) is sacred to the Navajos. It contains caprock of quartz sandstone resting on Mesozoic strata except at Chuska Peak, which is underlain by Tertiary shale and sandstone. On the west base of the mountains there are remnants of ancient volcanic action in the form of necks, dikes, lava flows, and layers of volcanic ash. Washington Pass (9,365') between Crystal and Sheep Springs has cliffs of tuff and shonkinite. The narrow pass was described by Lt. Simpson, whose military reconnaissance in 1850 traversed the mountains by this route. It is barely 50' wide, located between Simpson Creek and the Chaco drainage, and has 3-400' walls of volcanic rocks. The pass is named after Col. John M. Washington, Governor of New Mexico, 1848-49. Lava caps the mountains on both sides of the pass. The southern part of the Chuska Mountains including Todilto Park was surveyed and named by E. E. Gregory in 1917. His report on this fascinating region remained largely unkown in New Mexico and came to the attention of people there only when a Frenchman sent an inquiry years later. Since then, pictures of Venus Needle and Cleopatras Needle have been printed occasionally but the area seldom is visited.

The Navajo tribe now permits camping at the many rest areas

on its reservation and has provided improved campsites. Campers need to bring their own water in this arid land.

Todilto Park on Tohatchi quad is approximately 50 miles north of Gallup. It is reached from Fort Defiance, north of Window Rock in Arizona. The secondary road north of Fort Defiance along Black Creek leads back into New Mexico south of Red Lake (on Buell Park quad) past Zilditloi Mountain and eventually to Washington Pass. A fork of this road north of Split Mesa goes into Todilto (Tohdildonih) Park past Cleopatras Needle and Venus Needle to Beelzebub in the south part of the park.

The Black Creek valley has some rather unusual formations. At the foot of the dam at Red Lake is a volcanic neck more than 100' high, which is called "Outlet Neck." One mile southeast of Outlet Neck is another volcanic plug with striking features, a rounded ridge and a columnar pile with a 200' face, resembling a lion. This is called "The Beast."

Zilditloi Mountain (8,573') on the east side of the Black Creek valley is a flat dome of lava resting on sedimentary rocks which rises 1,400' above the plains. It was climbed by Gregory in 1917. The route from the west goes up a wall of sandstone, traverses a 0.5-mile wide bench, ascends a steep slope cut in sediments, and finally a steep 150' cliff of lava columns. The platform below the lava is nearly a mile wide on the east and north sides. The lava probably came from the necks in Todilto Park.

About 1.5 miles north of Red Lake on the road to Crystal there is a group of light green hills, the "Green Knobs," which contrast with the surrounding red sandstones. These are believed to represent a volcanic vent which is probably contemporaneous with the volcanic necks in the vicinity

The valley of Tohdildonih Wash at the entrance to Todilto Park is sometimes referred to as the Valley of the Obelisks. **Cleopatras Needle** on the west side is a slender sandstone shaft 213' high, named after the Egyptian obelisk in Central Park, New York City, which was given to the United States in 1880. Just east of there in Bowl Canyon is another sandstone column 207' high called **Venus Needle.** These needles are on the Navajo Reservation where all technical climbing has been banned since 1970.

Along the south rim of Todilto Park at the east base of Zilditloi Mountain the cores of two volcanoes are exposed. The larger one, **Beelzebub,** is a 200' volcanic neck. The other is a 0.7-mile long dike with 7 pinnacles, 100-150' above the sandstone slopes at its base. The dikes and necks on the east side of the Chuska Mountains include Shiprock (7,178'), Ford Butte, and Bennett Peak (6,652'). They were mapped by Shales who found them to consist chiefly of monchiquite.

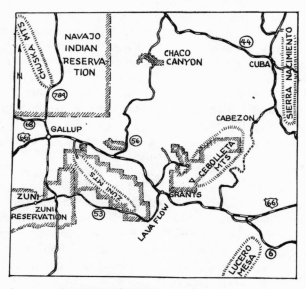

NORTHWESTERN NEW MEXICO

THE ZUNI MOUNTAINS

The Zuni Mountains south of U.S. 66 between Grants and Gallup are carved from a northwest-southeast uplift 60-80 miles long and 40 miles wide, composed of a Precambrian core and flanked by sediments ranging from Pennsylvanian to recent. The southern end of the range is complicated by faulting and obscured by lava. The uplift is of the plateau type. Near the town of Zuni it consists of light-colored sandstones with steep cliffs and deep canyons. The prominent Oso Ridge north of State Road 53 is covered with ponderosa pine and forms the continental divide. Mount Sedgwick, almost due west of Grants, is a granite mass.

Mount Sedgwick (9,256') the highest summit in the Zuni Mountains, is accessible by road from Grants. Drive up Zuni Canyon 17 miles to Ojo Redondo campground (9,000') and jeep or hike 1.5 miles north to the top. **Oso Ridge Lookout** (9,098') south of Mount Sedgwick is reached by a 3-mile dirt road from State Road 53. Another lookout on the northwest side of the mountains, **McGaffey Lookout,** is reached easiest by driving 10 miles south from U.S. 66 on State Road 400 through Fort Wingate to McGaffey campground (8,300') and continuing 3 miles to the top. There is also a 2.5-mile trail from the campground to the lookout. A secondary dirt road paralleling the Zuni Mountains on the north side connects Ojo Redondo with McGaffey campground. This road is open only during the summer. A small section of Cibola National Forest near the Zuni Mountains is north of U.S. 66 and is located on Indian land. The fire lookout on **Mount Powell** (8,743') in this section is open to the public and located 16 miles by road from U.S. 66 north of Thoreau.

The Zuni mountain region has a number of points of interest. It contains an ice cave 1 mile south of State Road 53 and nearby a crater (Bandera Crater), which is the same age as Sunset Crater in Arizona. El Morro National Monument (Inscription Rock) is on the south side of the Zuni Mountains, and the ruins of the historic pueblo of Zuni are on a steep-walled mesa, 1,200' above the plains, on the southwest side of the range. A steep sandstone mesa southeast of the present Zuni, named Taaiyalone (Corn Mountain), was used as a refuge by the Indians of the villages of Cibola in 1540 and again in 1635. It is still used for religious ceremonies by the Zuni Indians and may not be climbed.

THE CEBOLLETA AND SAN MATEO MOUNTAINS

The mountains northeast of Grants consist of a 44-mile long volcanic plateau topped by the large conical pile of Mount Taylor. In Spanish times, both the mesa and the mountain were named Cebolleta (tender onion). Later, the plateau was known as Mesa Chivato and the mountain was renamed for General Z. Taylor by a young officer from Santa Fe. Nowadays, the northern half of the mesa is called Cebolleta Mountains and the southern part, including Mount Taylor, the San Mateo Mountains. Mount Taylor is one of the sacred mountains of the Navajos.

The Mount Taylor volcanic field was first described by Captain C. Dutton in the sixth annual report of the U.S.G.S. of 1884-85 and mapped by C. B. Hunt of the U.S.G.S. in 1938. According to Dutton the mesa is Cretaceous material capped by 300' of lava sheets which came from successive outpourings from many vents. The top of the mesa is made up of basalt flows studded with numerous cinder cones. At the edge of the plateau weathering has eroded the lava cap and the softer layers beneath, leaving over 100 volcanic necks which are regarded as the feeders for the lava sheets. The necks are quite numerous in the Rio Puerco valley and on the south side of Mount Taylor. The few on the west side of the mountain are only a short distance from the mesa wall. Alesna, which is located on the Floyd Lee Ranch on the northwest side, is a steep butte composed of columnar basalt. The most famous neck is Cabezon in the Rio Puerco valley west of San Ysidro. The age of the Mount Taylor volcanic eruptions is estimated to be middle Tertiary and probably contemporaneous with the Jemez Mountains. The lava flows were much larger at one time and continuous with that of Mesa Prieta on the east side.

Mount Taylor (11,301′) on Mount Taylor quad can be climbed from La Mosca fire lookout (11,036′) by a 1-mile trail up the northeast ridge. To get to La Mosca summit from Grants, drive 4 miles northwest on U.S. 66, turn right (north) on State Road 53 and drive 22 miles to San Mateo. From there take Forest Service Road 51, 4 miles east and 53 south and west to the lookout. An alternate road from Grants, Forest Service Road 239, intersects 53 north of La Mosca. A trail from the saddle between Mount Taylor and La Mosca leads down Water Canyon and to a road at the forest boundary. This road runs through private ranches and is normally closed.

A number of the volcanic necks in the Mount Taylor volcanic field have been climbed. **Cabezon** is described in the climbing section. **Sonora Peak** in the Puerco valley, approximately 20 miles south of Cabezon, is usually reached from the south side. A dry weather dirt road goes up the Rio Puerco valley from U.S. 66, west of Albuquerque. **Alesna** (from la lesna, the awl) is on private property (Floyd Lee Ranch, where permission should be obtained). It has been called Shoemakers Awl and Sharks Tooth and was climbed in 1934 by Griswold and since then repeatedly by the New Mexico Mountaineers of Albuquerque. A picture of the peak is contained in Dutton's report of 1884-85.

Enchanted Mesa (Katzimo, haunted) is an isolated mesa with precipitous sandstone cliffs about 3 miles northeast of Acoma. The Acoma Indians shun the mesa. According to legend it was inhabited by some of their tribe long ago, when a storm wiped out the trail to the top. Of the three women who were stranded on the mesa, two died of starvation and the third jumped off.

The first attempt by Judd and Hodge in 1895 to climb the mesa near the southwest corner failed 60′ from the top, but they did find pottery in the talus slope. Professor Libby succeeded in climbing the mesa in 1897 stating that he found no evidence to substantiate the Acoma legend. However, Professor Hodge subsequently found crude ladder holes in the western face near the south end and discovered pottery and stone axes on the top. The mesa was climbed by other archaeologists, including Judd, Jordan, and Lummis, during the period from 1897 to 1907.

Enchanted Mesa stands 430' above the plain and the climbing route at the southwest corner is simple until one gets to the upper 60'. At this point a large vertical cleft leads up a steep sandstone buttress. Holes on both sides of the crack were used to hold wooden poles which then served as a ladder. These holes are now largely weathered and it is necessary to use direct aid and belays for the ascent.

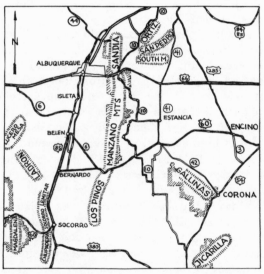

ALBUQUERQUE-SOCORRO REGION

THE ORTIZ AND SAN PEDRO MOUNTAINS

Three low dome-shaped uplifts east of State Highway 14 between Madrid and Tijeras are known as the Ortiz, San Pedro, and South Mountains. They are made up of laccolithic intrusions into volcanic rocks and Tertiary sediments. While these mountains are of little interest to climbers, they have been known longer perhaps than any other mountains in the state. Gold was discovered there first by the Spaniards in the 16th century. The use of Indian slave labor in the gold mines supposedly caused, at least in part, the Pueblo Revolt of 1680. The mines were hidden after the revolt and not rediscovered until 1828, when a Spanish sheepherder named Ortiz found gold near the former Dolores in the Ortiz Mountains. Gold was found also near San Pedro in 1832. These placers (gold-carrying gravels) were the first gold mining areas in the United States. They were visited by Dr. A. Wislicenus and Lt. J. W. Abert in 1846. A land grant was obtained by J. S. Ramirez in 1845. Other parts of the placers are on the Ortiz and San Pedro land grants. The area has yielded some 15 million dollars worth of gold, silver, lead, and zinc. The mother lode has never been found nor has the legendary Spanish "Cathedral Stope" been rediscovered, but remnants of original Spanish diggings have been found in the mountains.

The Ortiz Mountains are approximately half-way between Golden and Madrid. The highest summit on the northwest side near State Road 14 is Placer Mountain or Ortiz Peak (8,928'). The east-west range between Golden and San Pedro is called San Pedro Mountains and has two summits, San Pedro Mountain (8,242') and Oro Quay Peak (8,226'). South Mountain (8,748') and the smaller Monte Largo (7,606′) are parallel mountain ranges south of San Pedro.

THE SANDIA MOUNTAINS

The ridges northeast of Albuquerque between Tijeras (Spanish, scissors) Canyon and the foothills approximately 20 miles north are known as the Sandia (Spanish, watermelon) Mountains. They have a spectacular west face of Precambrian granite and a gradual wooded slope of Pennsylvanian limestone on the east side. A lower range in front of the main face on the west side is called the Rincon Ridge. It is connected to the mountains by a ridge which runs up to the North Peak. The valley between the ridges is referred to as the Juan Tabo area.

The Sandia Range is unique because it offers good hiking trails, an all-weather road to the top, and a number of fine climbing routes on good rock in the precipitous face. Sandia Cave on the east slope has yielded evidence of human occupations dating back some 20,000 years. To the much more recent Pueblo Indians, Sandia Peak and Rincon Ridge were sacred mountains. A shrine was maintained on Sandia Peak which was known as Oku Pin. Prayer sticks still are found occasionally on Sandia Crest. The entire range is now within Cibola National Forest and administered by the Forest Service; it is one of the regions in New Mexico where Rocky Mountain bighorn sheep are found at present. Recent developments include the Sandia Peak Ski Area and the highest television towers in the country. A cable car from the west side to the top of the ridge at a point about one mile south of Sandia Crest is in operation all year. The location at the edge of a big city has made outdoor recreation the fastest-growing use of these mountains. The Dolores treasure of gold coins, supposedly buried in the foothills east of Albuquerque under a grinding wheel, has not been found to date.

Sandia Crest (10,678′) on Sandia Crest quad is the highest point in the Sandia Mountains. It was climbed in 1853 by the Swiss geologist Jules Marcou who accompanied Lt. A. W. Whipple's reconnaissance party, which probably is the first recorded climb of a major peak in New Mexico. The crest can be reached by a modern highway from Tijeras Canyon, 8 miles east of Albuquerque. It is possible to hike to the top on the old La Luz trail from the Juan Tabo Recreation Area. This is the traditional New Year's Day hike of the New Mexico Mountaineers.

To get to the Juan Tabo picnic ground from the city, drive north on State Road 422 and turn east at Alameda or drive north on Juan Tabo Boulevard Extension on a gravel road which leads to the Juan Tabo Area at 6,700′. The 4.4-mile foot trail starts just south of the recreation area at a wooden marker. A trail with more gentle grades starting at the picnic grounds is now available to hikers. The remains of the La Luz Mine are found at 10,000′ near the old trail. The Thumb (10,107′), a rock formation of characteristic shape south of the old trail about 1 mile below the crest, can be climbed on a scree slope from the south side. The west and north faces of this rock are difficult climbs.

Among the climbing routes on the west side of the Sandia Mountains are: the Knife Edge, the Shield, the Prow, and the Needle. The Shield is the towering rock face overlooking the Juan Tabo bowl which contains the recreation area. A two-hour hike north of the picnic grounds leads to the start of the climb.

Sandia Peak, also called North Sandia Peak, (10,447′) is accessible by trail from Sandia Crest and is located 1.5 miles north on the ridge from there. The ridge trail continues north beyond the peak until it runs into an old jeep road which is no longer maintained. The ridge trail runs south from Sandia Crest 7 miles to South Sandia Peak and 8 miles farther to Carlito Springs near Tijeras Canyon. The new ridge trail now starts from a canyon between the State Road 14 intersections on the north side of Tijeras Canyon, rather than from Carlito Springs.

South Sandia Peak (9,782') on Tijeras quad may be climbed by the ridge trail, from Embudo, or Embudito Canyon. The Embudo trail goes through private property and permission is required to enter. The Embudito trail is reached from Montgomery Street, N.E. To climb the peak from the west, drive to Glenwood Hills Estates and hike east ¼ mile to the start of the trail. An alternate route by way of Cienega Canyon reaches the rim 4 miles south of Sandia Crest.

Sandia Cave. The ancient cave is near State Road 44 between Placitas and the junction of Sandia Crest Road. A 1.5-mile foot trail east of the road below Las Huertas (Spanish, "gardens") picnic ground (7,200') leads to the cave. The trail starting ¾ mile below the picnic ground is now available. The cave is being restored and there will be conducted tours in the near future.

For more information on the Sandias, technical climbers should refer to **Guide to the Sandia Mountains** edited by L. G. Kline (privately published, Albuquerque, 1970).

THE MANZANO MOUNTAINS

The 40-mile north-south mountain range between Tijeras Canyon and U.S. 60 is a continuation of the tilted fault block which contains the Sandia Mountains. It is named for the apple orchards which were planted around Manzano at 1800 and probably earlier. Manzano was settled about 1829, its houses clustered around the lake formed by the cold waters of the Ojo del Gigante (giant spring). The Spaniards operated silver and lead mines in the southern extremity of the Manzano Mountains. The smelter and various ore samples have been found, but the mine has not been located. It is believed to be in Priest Canyon. The location of the old "Holy Cross Mine" is given as northwest of Abo.

The Manzanita section of the Manzanos, immediately south of Tijeras Canyon, is a relatively low ridge within Cibola National Forest. An area on the west side is military reservation and closed to the public. The 8-mile section south of there is on the Isleta Indian Reservation with Guadalupe Peak as the highest point. The remaining portion of the range from just south of Guadalupe Peak to the vicinity of Abo Pass is again in Cibola National Forest.

Geologically these mountains are quite similar to the Sandias. In the Manzanita section Pennsylvanian layers lie nearly flat on the Precambrian granite. Farther south the strata are more tilted, the youngest layers have been eroded from the top, and the entire western face is Precambrian rock.

During the Pueblo period both sides of the mountains were inhabited, but the Pueblos Chilili, Tajique, and Torreon on the east side were abandoned during the 17th century because of Apache

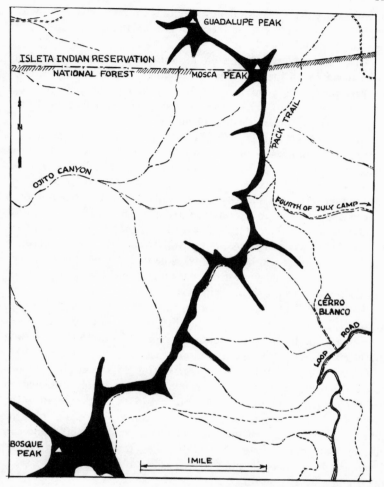

raids. An old Spanish road followed El Cañon Infierno (Hell
Canyon) through the Manzanos between Isleta and Escabosa (on
State Road 14). It was traveled in 1846 by Lt. J. W. Abert of the
U. S. Army, who described its rough condition. Tajique Canyon
on the east side and nearby Apache Canyon (and some canyons

in Sierra Blanca) are the only regions in New Mexico where
maple trees occur. The fall colors are particularly beautiful in
Tajique Canyon.

Most parts of the Manzano Mountains are approached from
State Road 14 on the east side of the range, as the access roads on
the precipitous west side are on Indian land or on private property. A road from Belen goes to the John F. Kennedy Picnic
Area in Trigo Canyon, north of Osha Peak.

Sol se Mete (Sunset) (7,541′) in the Manzanita section is
located on Mount Washington quad. Both Mount Washington
(7,716′) and Sol se Mete are within the Sandia Special Use Area
on an old artillery impact range, which is closed to the public. The
area extends from 5 miles south of U.S. 66 to the Isleta Indian
Reservation and east to within 1 mile of State Road 14.

Cedro (Spanish, cedar) **Peak** (7,767′) has a fire lookout on
its summit. One can drive to the top from State Road 14 on a
side road 5.5 miles south of U.S. 66 The distance on the secondary
road is 3 miles. The view from its summit includes much of the
Sandia and Manzano Mountain area.

Guadalupe Peak (9,450′) within the Isleta Indian Reservation,
is on Bosque Peak quad. It can be climbed by its north and southwest ridges or by a 1-mile scramble from Mosca Peak along the
southeast ridge. The loss in altitude between the peaks is 400′.
The west approach to the peak starts from Highway 47 just opposite the bridge over the Rio Grande at Isleta (route information
from Norman Bullard). The unpaved road runs through the
Isleta Reservation to within 3 miles of the peak. A fee may be
charged for entering. From the end of the road at 6,500′ one can
hike to the summit along a series of ridges topped with limestone.
There is no trail and the final stretch below the top goes up a talus
slope and through scrub oak.

Mosca (Spanish, fly) **Peak** (9,509′) is a little over ¼ mile
from the Manzano Crest trail. From the Tajique-Torreon Loop
Road drive northwest to the Fourth of July campground at 8,000′.
From there the trail goes west ¾ mile to the crest trail. Hike

north 0.5 mile to the saddle and scramble to the top through scrub oak along the ¾ mile south ridge of the peak.

Bosque (Spanish, forest) **Peak** (9,610′) is accessible by the same approach as Mosca Peak. Hike 2.5 miles south on the crest trail and scramble to the top from where the trail meets the sum-

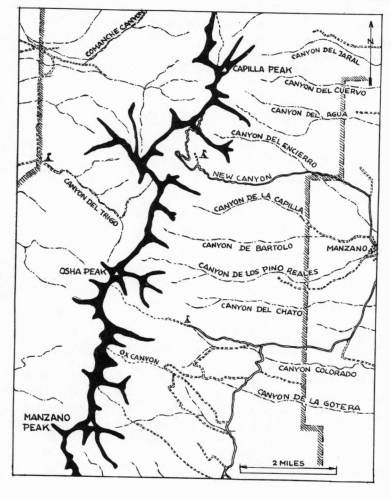

mit plateau. Continuing south on the crest trail 3.5 miles beyond Bosque Peak one can reach Capilla Peak (9,375'). This peak has a fire lookout and can be driven up on a 7-mile road from Manzano. Osha Peak (10,003') is 5 miles south on the crest trail from Capilla Peak.

Manzano Peak (10,098') on Torreon quad is the southern terminal of the long crest trail which extends into the Manzanita section. The shortest approach is from Red Canyon campground, which is on a road southwest of Manzano. A 2-mile trail leads west to the crest trail. From there it is 2 miles to the summit.

LOS PINOS MOUNTAINS

The southward extension of the Manzano Mountains south of Abo Pass on U.S. 60 is called the Los Pinos Mountains. The 25-mile long range is geologically similar to the Manzanos, having a west side composed of granite and overlaying sedimentary strata of Pennsylvanian and Madera formations. The two named summits are Whiteface Mountain (7,530') and Cerro Montosa (7,259').

THE GALLINAS MOUNTAINS

The Gallinas Mountains 50 miles east of the Los Pinos Mountains and directly west of Corona consist essentially of a domal uplift with Gallinas Peak (8,637′) as the highest point. This mountain is a laccolith which was formed by intrusion of granite into Permian rocks The main drainage is Redcloud Canyon on the southwest side of the mountain. This is the site of Redcloud campground (8,500′) and the former mining town of Redcloud. The iron and fluorite-copper mines in the canyon are largely abandoned and there is virtually no mining at present. To get to the Forest Service lookout on the peak drive 3 miles southwest from Corona on U.S. 54 and 12 miles west on a dirt road to the peak. North of Gallinas Peak and still within Cibola National Forest are the ruins of Pueblo Blanco and Pueblo Colorado.

THE LADRON MOUNTAINS

These mountains (Sierra Ladrones, Spanish—mountain of thieves), southwest of Albuquerque, on Riley quad, were once a meeting place for Navajo and Apache horse thieves. La Cueva de

Ladrones (the cave of thieves) southwest of Ladron Peak was at one time a refuge of bandits. The mountains are part of the Lucero uplift, which includes Gallina Mesa (7,840′) and Lucero Mesa (6,500′) farther north. The east side of the Ladron Mountains consists largely of granite, quartzite, and other Precambrian rocks while the west side is flanked by more recent (Mississippian and Pennsylvanian) sedimentary strata. Some gold was found in these mountains in the late 1860s.

Ladron Peak (9,176′) (from information by Norman Bullard), the highest point in these mountains, is climbed easiest from the southwest side, which is accessible by road in dry weather. To get onto the dirt road to the mountain, turn off from U.S. 85 at Bernardo, drive south on the old road and west over the old steel bridge across the Rio Puerco, which is located ⅜ mile southwest of the junction of U.S. 85 and U.S. 60. A few hundred feet beyond the bridge a ranch road leads to the west. It passes through the Rocking-M Ranch, where several gates must be opened (and closed), and goes around the mountain. After passing the peak on the north side, the road continues southwest and south (and eventually to Riley and Magdalena), climbing a steep ridge. Faint jeep tracks which lead to the mountain from here may be followed to an abandoned ranch house (about 25 miles from Bernardo), where cars may be parked at 6,100′. A trail of sorts in an arroyo leads to the peak. The route to the summit goes up a long boulder slide to a notch just south of the summit. The last 200′ require careful choice of route. The mountain has been climbed also from the north side.

THE SOCORRO MOUNTAINS

The Rio Grande valley near Socorro is bordered on the west side by a low and nearly bare north-south mountain range, the Lemitar-Socorro-Chupadera chain. The west slope of this narrow fault block is largely composed of Teritary volcanic rocks. The underlying Pennsylvanian and Precambrian layers are exposed at the eastern face. The city of Socorro, 74 miles south of Albuquerque, is located just south of the ruins of the Piro Pueblo Teypana, where Oñate was hospitably received in 1598. In recognition of the aid received he named the settlement Socorro (succor), which name was later applied to the present city and the mountains west of there between Nogal Canyon on the north, and Socorro Canyon (Highway 60) on the south. The northern extension of these mountains is known as the Lemitar Mountains and the range south of U.S. 60 as the Chupadera Mountains.

Archaeological evidence indicates that the Socorro region had prehistoric inhabitants belonging to the Folsom, Cochise, Basketmaker, and Pueblo cultures. The ancient people used chalcedony and jasper outcrops in the mountains and gravels along the river as raw material for the artifacts which have been found in the area. The Piro Indians who lived along the Rio Grande until Spanish times left during the Pueblo Revolt in 1680 because they did not partake in the revolt and feared retributions. The few who remained were wiped out by Apache. The region was resettled by Spanish families under a grant in 1817. Silver was discovered in 1867, and Socorro became the largest city in New Mexico in 1880 during the mining boom which lasted until 1890.

The mines in Socorro Mountain alone yielded one million dollars worth of silver.

The Lemitar and Chupadera mountains offer little of interest to mountaineers. The Lemitar range has two named summits, Polvadera Mountain (7,292') on Lemitar quad in the north, and Strawberry Peak (7,012') in the southern part of the range.

Strawberry Peak can be climbed from the west side but the steep northwest face should be avoided.

The Socorro Mountains have a prominent summit marked with the letter "M" near the top. This is **Socorro Peak** (7,243') on Socorro quad. The Socorro School of Mines (established in 1890) maintains laboratories on the mountain and access is restricted. Arrangements to enter the area must be made with the school. A good surfaced road leads to installations in Blue Canyon and a jeep trail from there to the crest of the peak, total distance, 6 miles. The steep 2,000' east face of the mountain was climbed by T. E. Dabney in 1947. The highest summit of the Socorro Mountains is an unnamed peak ¼ mile northwest of Socorro Peak with an altitude of 7,284'.

The Ladron-Socorro mountain area has the distinction of being the earthquake center of New Mexico. Epicenters are under Socorro Mountain and the Sierra Ladrones, the former having the higher levels. The seismograph station at the base of Socorro Mountain records an average of 2-3 quakes a day, most of which are very weak. Earthquakes have been observed in the region since 1855, but probably occurred much earlier. There is presumably underground magma in the area because tunnels some 400' below the surface at the base of Socorro Mountain have temperatures of 95°F and the thermal springs, which have been used as water supply since pre-Spanish times, measure 90-91°F.

THE BEAR, GALLINAS, AND DATIL MOUNTAINS

These mountains are taken up together because they are located in the same area, at the northern end of the Mogollon Plateau, are all in the Cibola National Forest, and have similar compositions. A group of low hills north of Magdalena comprises the **Bear Mountains.** They are composed of Tertiary volcanic rocks and rise to an elevation of 8,300′. Three bare volcanic buttes just north of U.S. 60 and 12 miles west of Magdalena are known as **Tres Montosos.** The highest of these is 8,550′ and rises 1,500′ above the plain.

The mountains directly north of these buttes are called **Gallinas Mountains** (not to be confused with the Gallinas Mountains in Lincoln County). These, too, are composed of volcanic rocks. They have three named summits, Gallinas Peak, Niggerhead (7,400′), and Table Mountain (7,000′).

Still farther west and directly north of Datil are the **Datil Mountains** which consist of tuff, conglomerate, and sandstone. The highest point is Madre Mountain (9,585′). A summit close to this mountain, named Davenport Peak (9,355′), has a fire lookout which can be reached by a steep 12-mile gravel road from U.S. 60 west of Datil. The western extension of the Datil Mountains is a low ridge, known as **Sawtooth Mountains** (8,950′). **Crosby Mountain** (9,000′) south of U.S. 60 is accessible by trail from a Forest Service road which connects U.S. 60 with State Road 12. D-Cross Mountain (8,400′), La Cruz Peak (6,975′), and La Jara Peak (6,875′) are volcanic necks north of the Gallinas Mountains. D-Cross Mountain derives its name from rock formations in the form of the letters D and X.

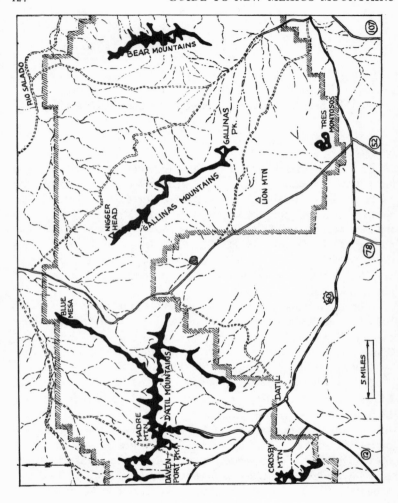

THE GALLO AND MANGAS MOUNTAINS

These mountains in Apache National Forest are small adjacent east-west mountain ranges between U.S. 60 and State Road 12 at the northwestern edge of the Mogollon Plateau. State Road 32 between Quemado and Apache Creek traverses the Gallo Mountains at Jewett Gap (8,500'). A side road leads to Fox Mountain (8,950'), 3 miles west of the gap. Other summits in the range are Apache Mountain (8,820') and Tularosa Mountain.

Mangas Mountain (9,650') in the Mangas mountain range is a Forest Service lookout which can be reached by the 12-mile road from Horse Springs on State Road 12. The continental divide runs over a part of the range, including Mangas Mountain, and intersects State Road 12 at an elevation of 7,312'.

THE MOGOLLON VOLCANIC PLATEAU

This area, about 100 miles in diameter, was formed 25 to 40 million years ago during a period of great volcanic activity in the southern part of New Mexico. It includes the Mogollon, San Francisco, Long Canyon, Tularosa, Elk, Saliz, Kelly, Jerky, Diablo, and Pinos Altos mountains. All of these consist of lava flows, tufa, ashes, pumice, and other volcanic materials. The main part of this plateau is in the Gila National Forest, a smaller area in the Gila Wilderness (the name Gila is supposedly an Indian word meaning spider), and the northwest corner in Apache National Forest. Most of this region was once Apacheria, the land of the Apache Indians.

The Mogollon Mountains in the southwest corner of Catron County and on the west side of the plateau, are named for Don Juan Ignacio Flores Mogollon, Governor of New Mexico from 1712-15. They are in the Gila National Forest and can be found on Mogollon quad.

Ruins on the mesas overlooking Whitewater Canyon and elsewhere in the mountains indicate that the region was inhabited in early times. The culture which thrived there beginning with the Christian era is in fact named after the mountains. Like most of the other southwestern mountain ranges, the Mogollons were Apache territory and Whitewater Canyon reputedly sheltered Geronimo.

In 1850 an explorer named Aubrey discovered gold in these mountains, but his discovery evidently was forgotten. During the mapping of the mountain area in 1870, Sgt. James Cooney from Ft. Bayard found gold quartz rock around the present village of

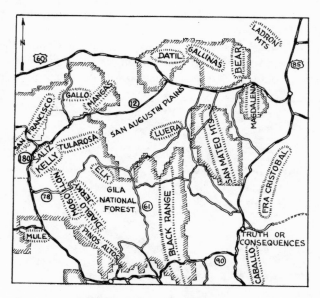

MOGOLLON PLATEAU

Mogollon. On his discharge in 1878 he opened a mine in the vicinity which he operated with two buddies. Apache Indians killed him, and he is buried along Mineral Creek, covered with ore from his mine. Other miners came into the region in 1880, Mogollon grew to a town of 2,000 inhabitants, and the mines yielded 20 million dollars in gold and silver For a time White-water Canyon was the hideout of "Butch" Cassidy and his Wild Bunch.

Nowadays two roads cross the Mogollon Mountains. State Road 78 continues from the ghost town of Mogollon (8 miles east of Alma) over the Silver Creek Divide into the Gila River valley. North of Alma on U.S. 180 a jeep road goes up Copper Canyon and across the divide 1 mile south of **Bearwallow Mountain** fire lookout (9,920'). A fork goes north on the ridge to the top of the lookout, another south from there on the top of the ridge to connect with State Road 78.

From Glenwood on U.S. 180 one can drive northwest into
Whitewater Canyon as far as Whitewater campground (4,800′)
and the "catwalk," a spectacular narrow walk built along the cliff
into the canyon. Water from the canyon was once piped to an ore
mill near the old town site of Graham below the campground. The

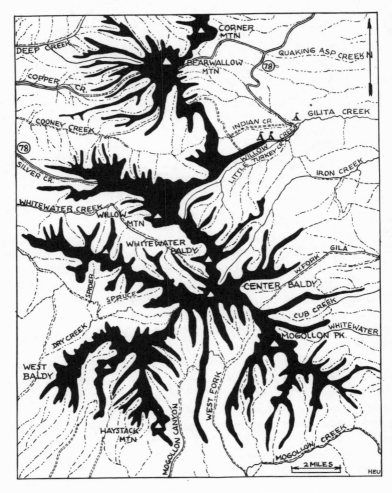

pipeline ran along the canyon wall, and the catwalk was built to maintain it. The pipe was sold in 1917, but the catwalk was rebuilt, finally with steel.

Whitewater Baldy (10,892′) and **Willow Mountain** (9,993′) can be climbed by the ridge trail from Sandy Point (8,500′) on State Road 78. The distance is 5 miles. The trail continues south to **Center Baldy** (10,532′), 1 mile, and **Mogollon Peak** or Mogollon Baldy, (10,778′), 6 miles. The latter, although a Forest Service fire lookout, can be reached only by pack trail. It is said to be the southernmost sacred mountain of the Navajo, who visited this region many years ago. **Grouse Mountain** (10,132′) is approximately 8 miles by trail from Whitewater campground. Other campgrounds are found along Willow Creek on State Road 78 at 8,100′.

The large expanse of the Mogollon Plateau north and east of the Mogollon Mountains, mostly in the Gila National Forest (on Reserve, Pelona, Mogollon, and Alum Mountain quads), from the Plains of San Augustin in the north to the Silver City region in the south, is drained by the Gila and San Francisco Rivers and carved by deep canyons into many small mountain ranges, individual mountains, and mesas. These are listed briefly in the following, with altitudes, named summits, and other significant data.

Starting in the north: the San Francisco River follows the Luna Valley east between Hellroaring Mesa (8,145′) and the San Francisco Mountains (8,435′) to a bend in the San Francisco Box Canyon south of Dillon Mountain (8,740′). From there it flows south past Reserve between the Saliz Mountains (7,576′) on the west side and the Tularosa Mountains (Eagle Peak, 9,802′) on the east side. The continental divide enters the area in the Long Canyon Mountains, running over John Kerr Peak (8,862′), south over Pinon Knob (8,677′) to the Elk Mountains (Elk Mountain, 9,780′). Then it skirts O-Bar-O Mountain (9,410′) on the north side and heads east over Pelona Mountain (9,204′), and just south of the Luera Mountains (Luera Peak, 9,420′) to the Black Range. South of the Elk Mountains in the center of the Gila Valley is the large circular Black Mountain

(9,303'). The Kelly Mountains (7,650') are on the east side of the San Francisco River gorge and just south of the Saliz Mountains. On the east side of the Mogollons are the small Jerky Mountains and Lilly Mountain (9,934') and the Diablo Range with Granny Mountain and Granite Peak (8,699'). The only named mountain range west of the Mogollons is the small Mule Mountain range 10 miles south of Pleasanton.

The Gila National Forest occupies an area once used as grazing land. A few families (for instance, the Shelly family) grazed cattle in the southern part while the northern section was sheep range. The region can be entered from U.S. 180 on the west and south and from State Roads 12, 25, 78, and 61 elsewhere. State Roads 78 and 61 cross a large part of the plateau. Secondary roads lead to the Forest Service lookouts on John Kerr Peak (8,862'), Eagle Peak (9,802'), Bearwallow Mountain (9,920'), Negrito Mountain (8,598'), Boiler Peak (8,048'), and Signal Peak. Other lookouts which can be reached only by trail are: Grouse Mountain (10,132'), Mogollon Baldy (10,778'), and Granite Peak (8,699').

One can drive from Pinos Altos north to the Gila Cliff Dwellings National Monument on State Roads 25 and 527. The new paved road in Copperas Canyon goes past the Gila Hot Springs and crosses the river twice. Available to the public are the Park Service and Forest Service museums. From the monument a network of trails leads to all parts of the wilderness. Trails in the northern part of Gila National Forest go along the ridge of the Tularosa Mountains, in the river gorge between the Saliz and Kelly Mountains, around the Kelly Mountains, and in the Deep Creek Valley northwest of Bearwallow Mountain. Campgrounds are found along routes 25, 61, and 78.

Some of the more popular trails in the Gila Wilderness have been given names. The McKenzie Trail (No. 6151) leads from Willow Creek to the White Creek Ranger Station; the West Fork Trail leads along the fork with this name. A trail going north from the West Fork is called the Zigzag Trail and the Sycamore

Trail (No. 6158) runs from Turkey Creek to the White Creek Ranger Station.

The San Francisco Mountains (on Reserve quad) in Apache National Forest consist of a northeast-southwest ridge touching the western border of New Mexico south of Luna. U.S. 180 crosses this wooded range between Reserve and Luna at an elevation of 8,010'. A rough road from the pass leads 15 miles southwest to Saddle Mountain lookout (8,200'). A trail northeast of the pass runs along the entire ridge to the San Francisco River Box.

The Pinos Altos (Tall Pines) **Mountains** 12 miles north of Silver City are part of the Mogollon Volcanic Plateau and composed chiefly of Miocene volcanic rocks. The small northwest-southeast range rises to an altitude of 9,025' at Black Peak.

Placer gold was discovered at Pinos Altos by Birch, Snively, and Hicks, prospectors from a party of California miners in 1860, and a vein deposit by Thomas Marston in the same year. Apaches raided the new settlement for some time until an agreement was made with them. After the Civil War in 1867 both placer and lode mining was continued, reaching a peak in 1868. There were once 75 arrastras and the gold, silver, copper, lead, and zinc produced by 1929 was valued at 8 million dollars. Water for the Pacific Mine was piped from a spring (Pine Cienega) in Cameron Creek Basin east of the Twin Sisters Canyon.

The continental divide runs over Black Peak and Twin Sisters (8,340'). Trails along this ridge are not maintained. State Road 25 crosses the mountains north of Pinos Altos. There are two campgrounds in Cherry Creek Canyon on the south side and a picnic ground at Lake Roberts. A scenic trail on the top of the ridge runs west from the Redstone Cabin 8 miles north of Pinos Altos, past Tadpole Lake to the Isabel Cabin (9 miles). Signal Peak (9,001'), the Forest Service fire lookout, can be reached by jeep road from the divide.

THE BLACK RANGE

The Black Range (also called Sierra de los Miembres, Sierra Diablo, or Devil Mountains) on the western border of Sierra County is a narrow north-south range nearly 100 miles long extending from near the San Augustin Plains to Thompson Cone. The Mimbres Mountains at the southern end are now considered a part of the range. From Reeds Peak north, the continental divide runs along the top of the ridge. The major part of the range is in Gila National Forest and a large section, in the Black Range Primitive Area.

The Black Range has a central core of Precambrian granite overlain by sediments and covered, especially on the west side, with layers of volcanic rocks which reach a thickness of 3,000'. The sequence is disturbed by various intrusions.

Numerous ruins in the Mimbres Valley and elsewhere identify the earliest settlers as Mogollons. It has been postulated that their descendents were wiped out by Apache who then claimed the area until territorial times as one of their favorite hunting grounds. One of Geronimo's trails to his hideouts ran through the Black Range above Chloride.

Lt. W. H. Emory, guided by Kit Carson, crossed the range in 1846 with the Army of the West at a pass which now carries his name. Very likely the Spaniards used it before him. Gold and silver was discovered in the Hillsboro district in 1877; silver at Lake Valley in 1878, near Chloride in 1879, and in the Kingston area in 1880. The new mining settlements on the east side of the mountains thrived in spite of Apache raids, and a mining boom developed which lasted for over 10 years. The most remarkable discovery was perhaps the "Bridal Chamber" near Lake Valley, an underground room which produced more than three million dollars in pure silver, so easy to mine that it could be loaded directly into railroad cars. It was during the mining years in 1888 on Thanksgiving that one Captain Crozier was surprised by a snowstorm on the top of the Black Range. The story goes that he disembowled his horse when it died and crawled inside, staying three days and nights. He survived but froze most of his toes.

Tin deposits in the Black Range were known to the prehistoric Indians because their burials contained tin stone beads drilled with quartz crystals. Cassiterite (stream tin) was rediscovered in the Taylor Creek district on the northwest side of the range in 1918. It occurs in small veins in the volcanic material of the Mogollon Plateau. The deposits are shallow and have yielded only small quantities of tin.

The mountains are traversed by State Roads 59 and 90 and the main ridge is accessible by various side roads from the Rio Grande and Mimbres Valleys.

Lookout Mountain (8,872'), on Lookout Mountain quad, is a fire lookout in Gila National Forest and has a road to the top from the west side connecting with State Road 61.

Diamond Peak (10,011') and **Reeds Peak** (10,012') can be climbed from State Road 52. Drive south from Winston on a gravel road to Hermosa (7,200') and climb northwest along Rattlesnake Creek to the top of the ridge. Diamond fire lookout is 3 miles north on the ridge trail and Reeds Peak is 4 miles south. An alternate route starts from State Road 61, 6 miles north of Mimbres. Take the Forest Service road opposite Camp Thunderbird northeast to the divide and hike north 8 miles to Reeds Peak.

Hillsboro Peak (10,011'), on San Lorenzo quad, is accessible from the east side from a side road which turns north from State Road 90, 2 miles east of Kingston. A trail leads west and southwest up Mineral Creek to the divide just south of the peak. An alternate route from the Mimbres Valley can be used, but the shortest approach is the 5-mile ridge trail from Emory Pass (8,178') over Cross-O Mountain (9,619'). Campgrounds are available along State Road 90 on the west side of Emory Pass. The ridge trail starts from the headwaters of Chloride Creek, west of the ghost town of Chloride, intersects State Road 90 at the pass, and continues south past Thompson Cone (7,932') to the Berenda Creek Valley.

Sawyers Peak (9,668'), named for an engineer Sawyer, is 4 miles south of Emory Pass on the ridge trail.

THE BURRO MOUNTAINS

The mountain ranges with this name, the Big and Little Burro Mountains, are parallel ranges southeast of Silver City. The Mangas Valley separates the two, the little Burro Mountains lying east and the Big Burro Mountains on the west side of the valley.

The Little Burro Mountains are only 8 miles long and mostly on private property. They consist of Precambrian rocks capped with quartzite and have one bare summit, Bald Mountain (6,396').

The Big Burro Mountains are in the Gila National Forest and can be found on Cliff, Redrock, Wind Mountain, and Big Burro Mountain quads. They represent a Precambrian batholith. The Precambrian southwest flank is overlain by Paleozoic and Mesozoic sediments. The wooded range is more than 20 miles long and rises to an elevation of 8,035' at Burro Peak. The continental divide touches the east slope of the Little Burro Mountains and runs over Burro Peak and a shoulder of Jacks Mountain in the Big Burro Mountains.

Turquoise deposits in the Big Burro Mountains were worked by the prehistoric Indians. An ancient shaft was found in 1900 which had been filled with heavy black dirt foreign to the region. The ancient workings were rediscovered in 1875 by John Coleman, who found a stone axe, red pottery, and diggings to the west of St. Louis Canyon. He talked so much about his discovery that he became known as "Turquoise John." Various mines were operated in the ensuing years along St. Louis Canyon. The Elizabeth pocket in the Azure Mine, a 40' x 60' vein, alone produced two

million dollars worth of turquoise. Other mines in the mountains
have yielded copper, gold, silver, maganese, and fluorite in small
amounts. The main deposits are nearly exhausted and there is
little mining now. The model town Tyrone and the adjacent Leopold just west of State Road 90 have become ghost towns.

The summits in the northern end of the mountains are **School-
house Mountain** (6,370′), **Wild Horse Peak** (6,078′), and **Bullard
Peak** (or Bullard Cone) (7,064′). The latter is named for Captain
John Bullard, one of the discoverers of Chloride Flat. Bullard
was shot and killed in 1871 on the slope of another peak with the
same name west of Glenwood, just over the Arizona state line,
when he stood over a presumably dead Apache. Native silver ores
have been found near the Bullard Peak in the Burro Mountains.

There are many old mine roads in these mountains. A Forest
Service road crosses the range south of Bullard Peak, and a jeep
side road runs close to the west side of the peak. Another Forest
Service road goes into the mountains southwest from Tyrone and
crosses the divide into Thompson Canyon. The southern summits,
Burro Peak (8,035′), **Jacks Mountain** (7,986′), and **South Peak,**
can be reached from the road which goes from State Road 90 to
the site of the former Solar Radiation Laboratory of the Smith-
sonian Institute on South Peak, now occupied by radio and TV installations. **Knight Peak** (6,602′) in the southern part of the Burro
Mountains, on Red Rock quad, can be reached by a secondary
road which ascends Knight Canyon from State Road 90 to within
a mile of the peak. The mountain is located at the Malone Fault,
in a region of Quarternary sediments and conglomerates. It can
be climbed via the southwest face on a series of five benches.

COOKS RANGE

Cooks Range (also Cookes Range), a mountain range south of the Black Range and 20 miles north of Deming, has one prominent summit, Cooks (Cookes) Peak (8,404'). It was named for Philip St. George Cooke who was in command of the Mormon caravan in Kearny's army in 1847. The mountain is located northwest of the ruins of Fort Cummings (1863-86). Both can be approached on a primitive road from Florida on State Road 26.

For centuries the range was in Apache territory and was used as a lookout because of its commanding position. The Butterfield stage was routed around the steep side of this mountain because several springs furnished water, the most important being Cookes Spring at the eastern edge of Cookes Canyon which was used as a watering stop. Soldiers were detailed as guards while the road was built up the main canyon. Frequent attacks on travelers at the spring or in the 4 miles of Cookes Canyon led to the establishment of Fort Cummings at the spring.

Mineral was found on Cooks Peak by Edward Orr in 1876. The lead-silver ore was hauled down the wagon road and earned several million dollars. While the mines were active there was a settlement on the peak. It had a post office and Jim McKenna was postmaster and judge.

A mountain southeast of Cooks Peak is called Massacre Peak because a wagon train from Juarez was ambushed there by Victorio and his band in 1879. The victims are buried in a common grave at the base of the peak.

THE SAN MATEO MOUNTAINS

The mountains between the Magdalena Mountains and the Black Range extend 46 miles from the Plains of San Augustin to the Rio Grande Valley west of Elephant Butte Reservoir. The forested ridges are in Cibola National Forest and the once over-grazed area again supports deer, antelope, and wild turkeys. The mountains consist of Tertiary volcanic rocks which rise some 4,000' above the valley floor. Steep cliffs are found in the upper reaches of the canyons while the lower valleys have gentle slopes.

The San Mateo Mountains were hunting ground and refuge for the Apache Indians, particularly Victorio, for whom Vicks Peak is named. Old cartridges and graves have been found at the base of this peak. During the mining rush which followed the Apache wars, gold, silver, and copper were found in the mountains, particularly in Rosedale Canyon, around Vicks Peak, and in the Goldsboro district on the southwest side of the mountains. There is little left of the ghost town of Rosedale, and the mines on the south side of the mountains have never yielded great riches. Hot springs on the west slope of the San Mateos near Ojo Caliente are remnants of ancient volcanic activity.

Mt. Withington (10,116') lookout is 16 miles south of U.S. 60. The road to the top starts up the mountain from State Road 52 in Beartrap Canyon. From the summit one can drive 6 miles south along the ridge to **Grassy** lookout (9,679') and return the same way, or through Rosedale Canyon to State Road 107. The peaks south of Grassy are accessible by trail. Thus, one can hike approximately 5 miles south from Grassy to Mulligan Peak. **Blue Mountain** (10,325') is 5 miles by trail from the end of the road in West Red Canyon. To reach **San Mateo Peak** (10,141′) take the 3.5-mile trail from Springtime campground on the southeast side of the range. The grave of the Apache Kid is on the ridge north of San Mateo Peak, and a summit north of there bears his name. **Vicks Peak** (10,290′), 4.5 miles south from San Mateo Peak, is close to the trail in Shipman Canyon which turns off from

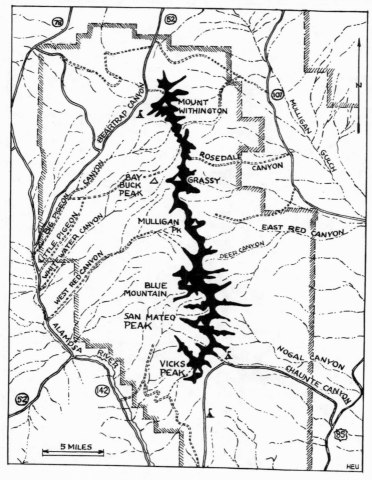

the secondary road between State Road 142 and the Forest Service road from Monticello to Springtime campground. The distance to the peak is approximately 3 miles. Springtime campground (7,500') is 17 miles northwest from U.S. 85.

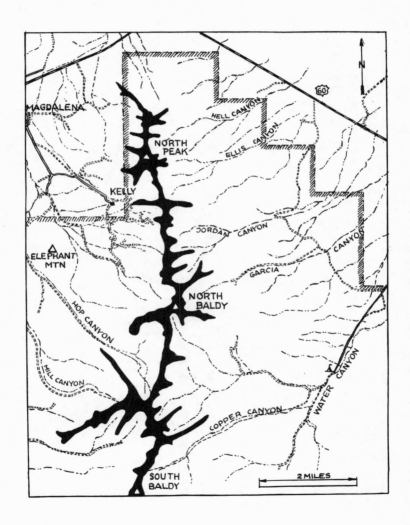

THE MAGDALENA MOUNTAINS

This small north-south mountain range lies south of U.S. 60 and just west of the Socorro region. It is located in Cibola National Forest and most of the area can be found on Magdalena quad. The core of the mountains is granite, overlain with limestone and covered partially, particularly in the southern part, by Tertiary volcanics. There is an almost bare volcanic mountain on the west side of the range which has on its eastern slope the profile of a woman's face (Magdalena Peak, 8,152'). This mountain was sacred and a sanctuary to the Indians. It was named for Mary Magdalena by the Spaniards and the name was then given to the whole range. Ore deposits were discovered on the west side of the Magdalena Mountains about 1866 when J. S. Hutchason filed claims for the Graphic and Juanita mines. The town of Magdalena (5,575') was founded in 1884 by miners who worked small claims in spite of frequent Apache raids. Kelly, south of Magdalena, is now a ghost town. It was the center of the mining district which yielded gold, silver, zinc, and lead—one mine alone giving ore valued at 30 million dollars. The Kelly mines were bought in 1913 by the Empire Zinc Company and operated until 1922. The combined Waldo-Graphic mines resumed operation in 1926.

The two major summits in the range, North and South Baldy, are now easily accessible as the School of Mines at Socorro maintains a laboratory on a peak approximately 1 mile south of South Baldy and a road in Water Canyon. The Forest Service campground in the canyon is open all year.

South Baldy (10,640'). The School of Mines road to the

Atmospheric Research Laboratory starts from U.S. 60 and goes through Water Canyon 14.2 miles to the top. The road skirts the southeast side of South Baldy only a short distance from the top. From the summit a 4-mile trail along the ridge leads to North Baldy (9,858′). The high central ridge in the northern part can be reached also from any one of several mine roads in the canyons on the west side of the mountains, for instance, from Hop Canyon, Mill Canyon, or from Kelly.

THE FRA CRISTOBAL RANGE

Together with the Caballo Mountains, this range forms an almost continuous bare mountain chain on the east side of the Rio Grande between Hatch and San Marcial. The 20-mile Fra Cristobal Range east of Elephant Butte Reservoir rises to an elevation of approximately 6,600′. The only named summit is Fra Cristobal Mountain in the northern half. The entire range is within the boundaries of the Pedro Armendaris land grant. A geological survey, made for the owners, showed no mineral deposits of interest, although Pedro de Abalos registered a gold mine in 1685 believed to be in these mountains. Some Precambrian granites crop out at the foot of the western face. These are overlain by thick Paleozic sequences dipping east, most of the face consisting of Magdalena limestone. On the eastern slope are several large limestone caves with millions of bats. The guano from these caves has been shipped out on several occasions.

THE CABALLO MOUNTAINS

The Caballo Mountains (Sierra Caballos, Spanish, Horse Mountains) just south of the Fra Cristobal Range are structurally similar. The tilted fault block has gentle east slopes and a steep western face. Precambrian rocks are exposed at the base of the west face while the main part of the range consists of limestone and other sediments. The mountains are divided into two parts by a pass in the middle of the range called Palomas Gap, named for the doves which lived in the cottonwoods along the river. The divide north of the Gap is called North Ridge and has one major summit, Caballo Cone, across the river from Truth or Consequences. South Ridge rises to 7,300' at the highest point, Timber Mountain. Other breaks in the long ridge are Granite Wash and Burbank Canyon.

Lt. Zebulon Pike noted in his report that he was taken by the Spaniards in 1807 on a route around the west side of these mountains, which took five days rather than the two days normally required for the route through the Jornada del Muerto. He passed the west side of "Horse Mountain" on the way to the Santa Rita Mine.

Placer gold was discovered in 1901 at Shandon near the southern end of the range by Encarnacion Silva, and the deposits became known two years later when Silva disclosed the location of his diggings at Hillsboro. The main deposit was mined in 1904-05, and during this time some lead and copper were found in the range. A toll road was built through Palomas Gap in 1907, and a few years later vanadium and lead ore were mined in the Gap. More recent mining in the mountains was for fluorspar which occurs in the limestone.

The most important event in the region was the building of Elephant Butte and Caballo dams for irrigation. Caballo Reservoir closed off the Palomas Gap road. The fluorspar mines in the northern end of the mountains are now reached by way of U.S. 52 from Truth or Consequences, as is the east side of the range. A road from State Road 140 east of Hatch follows an arroyo into Palm Park near Red House Mountain. Tipton Ranch near Nakaye Mountain on the west side of the range is reached by a dirt road in Green Canyon near Derry. This connects with the road from Caballo Dam through Apache Canyon (see Upham quad).

Caballo Cone (6,091'), on Eagle quad, is the summit of Turtle Mountain (also called Turtle Back or Turtle Top) on the northern tip of the range. There is a trail on the ridge which goes over this summit and to another directly south which is called **Caballo Mountain** (5,993') locally. Water is scarce in these mountains and should be carried.

THE PICACHO-ROBLEDO RANGE

This range is sometimes referred to as Selden Mountains.

Picacho Peak (4,954'), northwest of Las Cruces, and on the southern end of this fault block range, is made up of volcanic material, while Robledo Mountain consists of sandstone and limestone. The Butterfield trail crossed the range via the second canyon north of Picacho Peak (Apache Canyon) after fording the Rio Grande at Mesilla.

Robledo Mountain (5,876') north of Apache Canyon was named for Pedro Robledo, a member of Oñate's Expedition of 1598, who was buried nearby. The mountain was used as a heliograph station by the U. S. Army to flash messages from Fort Selden to Fort Bliss at Franklin (El Paso, Texas) during the Apache campaigns and later as an astronomical station.

THE SIERRA DE LAS UVAS

Sierra de las Uvas (Spanish, Mountain of Grapes) (6,601'), on Souse Springs quad, is a dome-shaped circular formation 10 miles in diameter, south of Hatch and Northwest of Robledo Mountain. It has extensive areas covered with basaltic andesite. The volcanic formations are broken by many faults.

THE OSCURA MOUNTAINS

The long Oscura-San Andres mountain range is separated by Mockingbird Gap near the Trinity Site in the Missile Range. The Oscura (Spanish, dark) Mountains north of the gap dip east while the San Andres Mountains dip west. Both have thick layers of sedimentary rocks resting on Precambrian formations.

Copper was mined in the Oscura Mountains in Spanish times. Mining was resumed toward the end of the 19th century and a small town, Estey (Estes) City, on Mockingbird Gap quad, sprang up in the southern red foothills. Regular shipments of ore were smelted in El Paso until 1902, when the price of copper dropped, springs dried up, and the company went bankrupt. The mines were reopened in 1903 and wells were drilled but water remained scarce and the town died in 1910. The ore is not depleted. The Oscura mines have yielded also lead, barite, and fluorspar, which was milled near Socorro.

The steep western face of the Oscuras has two named peaks, North Oscura Peak (7,999′), on Bingham quad, and Oscura Peak (8,640′), on Mockingbird Gap quad. The entire range is in the Missile Range and permission is required to enter.

THE SAN ANDRES MOUNTAINS

These mountains between the Tularosa Plain and the Jornada del Muerto extend 80 miles from Mockingbird Gap (5,280') to San Augustin Pass (5,719'). They are 6-17 miles wide and drained by fourteen east-west canyons. Rhodes Canyon was traversed by the former State Road 52 from Engle to Tularosa. This road is now closed since the mountains are within the Missile Range and may be entered only with the permission of the commanding officer. Rhodes Canyon is the site of the Eugene Manlove Rhodes Ranch, and his grave is on top of Rhodes Pass (6,533'). He was a writer of authentic western stories and one of the first homesteaders in the San Andres.

The mountain range has a gentle west slope but a steep east scarp which rises nearly 3,000' above the Tularosa Basin. It has three peaks over 8,000' high: Greer Peak (or Silver Top Mountain) (8,005'), Salinas Peak (8,958'), and San Andres Peak (8,239'), and a number of lower summits, e.g., Bear Peak (7,055'), Capitol Peak (7,098'), Sheep Mountain and Soledad Peak. Passes not previously mentioned are: Hays Gap (5,240'), Lava Gap in Thoroughgood Canyon (5,270'), Hembrillo Pass (5,790'), and passes in Cottonwood Canyon (6,310'), Sulphur Canyon (5,920'), Dead Man Canyon (5,740'), San Andres Canyon (5,350'), Ash Canyon (5,820'), and Bear Canyon (5,795).

The lost mine on Soledad Peak is perhaps the most famous part of the range. According to legend, the gold mine of Padre La Rue was hidden and sealed when Spanish soldiers approached and the secret of its location died with the padre when he was murdered. A manuscript dated 1797 describes a location which

fits Soledad Peak. Doc Noss from Hot Springs supposedly rediscovered the mine in 1937, only to lose it when a cave-in blocked
the entrance. Other legends place the mine in the Organ Mountains but no evidence ever has been found there.

In the southern part of the San Andres Mountains just west
of Jornada Range Reserve is the San Andres National Wildlife
Refuge where desert bighorn sheep are protected. This refuge includes the San Andres Peak area. The peak can be climbed easily
from the road which parallels the mountains on the west side.
Permission is required as the area is in the Missile Range.

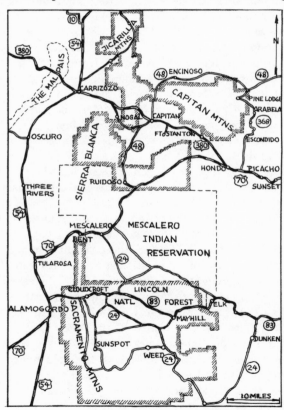

THE SACRAMENTO MOUNTAINS

Some maps label only the mountains south of U.S. 70 as Sacramento Mountains, but the U.S. Geological Survey designates the entire 90-mile mountain range from a point 40 miles north of the Texas border to the northern end of the Jicarillas as the Sacramento Mountains. This classification has been retained and the Jicarilla, Capitan, Sierra Blanca, and Sacramento Mountains are regarded as subranges. Single mountains such as Carrizo, Patos, and Tucson Mountains which stand apart from the subranges are included in the Sacramento range. The greater part of these mountains is in Lincoln National Forest.

Jicarilla Mountains. The northernmost mountains in the Sacramento range are the Jicarillas, 8 miles southeast of Ancho. The main mass of these mountains rises to an altitude of 7,900' and consists of intrusive quartz monzonite porphyry which crops out near the village of Jicarilla and at Jack's Peak. It is overlain elsewhere by various sediments.

Cowboys found placer gold in a gulch near Jicarilla in 1850 and during the following years some $90,000's worth was mined. The Jack Mines on the west side of Jack's Peak have furnished magnetite-hematite ore. Attempts have been made in the past to exploit abundant gypsum and clay deposits, but at present there is no mining in these mountains. Lack of water makes gold mining uneconomical.

The White Oaks mining district 10 miles south of the Jicarilla Mountains was centered around White Oaks Canyon northeast of Carrizozo, where the ghost town of White Oaks is located. The district was discovered in 1880 when three prospectors, Harry

Baxter, Jack Winters, and the desperado John Wilson, panned for gold in a gulch on Baxter Mountain(7,285') which is named for Harry Baxter. Wilson found gold in the canyon and all three staked claims. Since Wilson had a price on his head, he sold out to his partners, reportedly for nine silver dollars, a horse, and a gun. The mines in the gulch yielded much gold, particularly the Old Abe Mine. A rich vein in this mine was 1,400' deep and produced 3 million dollars' worth.

Gold-bearing strata along the Vera Cruz Mountain laccolith were mined in the early part of the present century. Other mines were in Lone Mountain, and iron as well as soft coal deposits were found east of White Oaks.

Mines southeast of Little Black Peak (5,679') on Little Black Peak quad, are usually included in the White Oaks district. They have furnished gold, tungsten, and iron ores. The peak is a little cinder cone located 8 miles north and slightly west of Carrizozo. It stands 85' above the plain and has a crater 32' deep. The malpais came from vents at Little Black Peak. Other basaltic flows northwest of the malpais probably came from vents near Broken Back Crater, 8 miles distant.

Capitan Mountains. Among the mountains east of Carrizozo; Carrizo, Vera Cruz, and the Capitan Mountains, consist of igneous rocks and can be classified as laccoliths (intrusions into sedimentary rocks) in which the original overlying sediments have been removed largely by erosion.

The Capitan Mountains farthest east from Carrizozo and just north of U.S. 380 are some 23 miles long but only 8 miles wide, unlike the usual laccolith which is round. The local Indian name for the Capitan range means "Mountain that stands alone," which describes its appearance from the east. The village of Capitan is probably named after the mountains, although some claim that it is named after a Captain Baca who settled there in 1868.

The mountain range is made up of two sections which are divided by a low pass, Capitan Gap (7,452') northeast of Capitan. The highest summit, Capitan Peak, is in the eastern portion. The wooded range had a disastrous fire in 1950 which burned the slopes. After the fire, a little bear cub was tound clinging to a tree, burned and hungry. It was nursed back to health and flown to the National Zoo in Washington, D. C., where it became the living symbol of Smokey, the forest fire-preventing bear of the U.S. Forest Service.

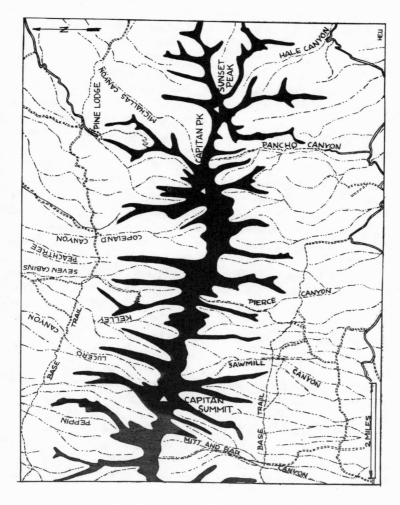

Commercial deposits of iron and thorium-bearing minerals have been found near West Mountain in the western section of the Capitans. Coal deposits west of Capitan were mined for a time at the turn of the century, but large reserves remain.

Capitan Peak (10,083'), on Capitan Mountain quad, can be climbed by a 6-mile trail from Pine Lodge. This trail continues beyond the peak along the ridge to Capitan Pass for a distance of about 14 miles. The last 7 miles from Capitan summit to the pass are now a service road for the repeater station on the summit. Parallel base trails run along the north and south sides of the mountains and the Pierce Canyon trail from the south traverses the ridge at Pierce Canyon Pass (9,242') to come out near the Fox and Fur Lodge in Seven Cabins Canyon on the north side. A portion of the northern trail east of Seven Cabins Canyon is now also a road.

West Mountain (8,842'), on Capitan quad, can be climbed from State Road 48 north of Capitan by a 2-mile trail from Jacob Spring on the northwest side. An old logging road on the south side of the mountain leads to the summit.

The three dome-shaped mountains between Carrizozo and the Capitan range north of U.S. 380, Tucson, Carrizo, and Patos Mountains, are found on Capitan quad.

Tucson Mountain (8,308') has an old road to the top. This is not maintained and very rough. The mountain can be climbed from the east side by the Tucson Mountain trail which starts from the National Forest boundary northwest of Capitan or from Bernado Canyon on the northwest side by using the Goat Springs trail which runs into the old road.

Carrizo Mountain (9,656') is climbed via the 4-mile Johnnie Canyon Trail on the southeast side or the 5.5-mile Water Canyon trail from White Oaks. A radio station on a shoulder of the mountain can be reached by road.

Patos Mountain (8,508') is accessible from the old wagon road between White Oaks and the Phillips Ranch and from the base trail on the north side. White Oaks Canyon may be driven 2 miles up to the old power plant and hiked 2.5 miles to the trail. From the base trail turn southeast on the 1-mile Trail Canyon trail which runs over the summit.

Sierra Blanca (White Mountains). The mountain range between Nogal Arroyo near Carrizozo and Tularosa Canyon is known as Sierra Blanca. It is a large extrusive volcanic pile made up of tuff, flows, and boulders, which has eroded from an even greater height to the present altitude of 12,003' at Sierra Blanca Peak. There is evidence that the higher parts of this range were glaciated during Pleistocene times. Petroglyphs in the foothills and pueblo ruins indicate early occupation of the region. The mountain was sacred to the ancient Indians and still is to the Apache whose reservation includes the southern part of the range. The Sierra Blanca region was Apache territory until American settlers arrived in 1862. The fertile Three Rivers Valley was settled in 1874 by Pat Coghlan, the "King of Tularosa."

Numerous intrusions of monzonite porphyry into the volcanic deposits account for the ore bodies which were mined on the east side of the range. Placer gold was first found in the vicinity of Nogal in 1865. Active prospecting began in 1882, and between then and 1916 more than one-half million dollars in ore were taken out of the Nogal district. Old mine workings are found in Nogal Canyon and even higher on the side of Nogal Peak (9,950').

Sierra Blanca Peak, Old Baldy, (12,003'), the highest peak in the range, can be climbed from the Sierra Blanca Ski Resort (9,700') which is owned and operated by the Mescalero Apache Indians. The distance is only 3 miles but the route is steep. From the ski resort one can take a gondola lift to the top of Lookout Peak (11,400'). The Sierra Blanca Ski Resort is 12 miles west of Alto on State Road 532. A pleasant 8-mile trail to the peak follows the ridge from Mon Jeau Lookout (10,000'), reached by a 12-mile road from Alto on State Road 37.

The Sierra Blanca Crest trail runs along the entire ridge of the mountains from Sierra Blanca to Nogal Peak, and numerous side trails lead to the Bonito Creek and Three Rivers valleys. Most of this high country is in the White Mountain Wild Area. Sierra Blanca is not only the highest mountain in southern New

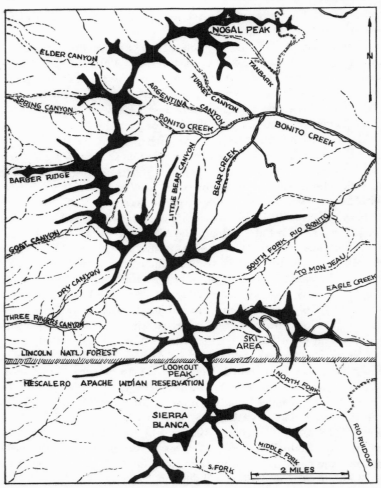

Mexico but also has the greatest relief of any peak in the state. It towers 7,800' above the Tularosa Valley.

Sacramento Mountains. South of Tularosa Canyon the mountains have the same name as the main range. The Sacramento Mountains rise in two steps to about a mile above the Tularosa plain. The crest near the west side of the tilted range is above 9,000' for a distance of over 20 miles. East of the crest the range slopes gradually toward the Pecos River about 80 miles away. The west side is carved into steep-walled canyons with cliffs of Pennsylvanian reef structures. These are overlain by Permian sediments. The 600' thick top layer of the range consists of San Andres limestone and is believed to carry water from the upper slopes to the Artesia region.

The Sacramento mountains were home, shrine, and hunting ground to the Apache. The famous "Eyebrow" trail in Dog Canyon (Cañyon del Perro) was the scene of many battles between Apache and troops, some occurring in 1859, 1863, and 1878. The old Apache Chief Nana resumed his war near there with only 15 men. Although rheumatic and almost blind, he fought 8 battles against nearly 1,000 men, killed an estimated 200, kidnapped two white women, stole over 200 horses, and escaped. In 1880, 60 soldiers followed him into Dog Canyon. When they were on the Eyebrow trail, the Indians rolled rocks on them and killed or injured most. The Peñasco Valley, although given to the Mescalero Apache Indians, was settled by Americans. The Indians finally accepted the smaller reservation which they now occupy.

A rail line with wooded trestles was built from Alamogordo into the Sacramento Mountains in 1898 for hauling timber. Excursion trains were run frequently and the resort area at Cloudcroft was opened in 1899. The railroad was abandoned in 1947. The U.S. Air Force maintains a solar observatory, named Sunspot, on Sacramento Peak (9,250'), 17 miles south of Cloudcroft on paved road.

Forest Service trails are found in Dog, Mule, and Alamo canyons. Each year in September the Alamogordo Chamber of Commerce sponsors a tour of Dog Canyon, on foot or horse. The trails connect with the Forest Service road from High Rolls on State Road 82. The 1.5-mile Tally trail from Cloudcroft leads to a viewpoint. For more extended hiking one can take the 6-mile scenic trail from Sacramento Peak to Hornbuckle Hill. Campgrounds are available near Cloudcroft and in Karr Canyon. Alamo Peak (9,685') is an old fire lookout.

THE GUADALUPE MOUNTAINS

This mountain range extending southeast from the vicinity of Piñon on State Road 24 into Texas is nearly 100 miles long. The highest summit, Guadalupe or Signal Peak (8,751'), which is in the triangular section in Texas, is also the highest point in that state. The Apache chief, Geronimo, used to say that the richest gold mines in the western world were hidden in the Guadalupes. A prospector, "Old Ben" Sublett, brought gold out of these mountains, but the secret of its location died with him. No one has found any more gold to date.

In New Mexico the narrow range consists of a long ridge, 6-7,000' high, called "The Rim." It has a steep 2,000' drop on the west side but slopes gently toward the Pecos Valley on the east side. The mountains represent an ancient reef structure of Capitan limestone which was formed some 300 million years ago and was raised during the Laramide Revolution.

The outstanding feature of the Guadalupe Mountains is the occurrence of numerous caves, the most famous being the Carlsbad Caverns on the east side which have become a National Park. The major area of the Guadalupe Mountains which is not included in the park is in Lincoln National Forest. Among the better known caves in this area are: Burnet Cave, Guadalupe Cavern, Lake Cave, Rainbow Cave, Painted Grotto, Cottonwood, Black, Hidden, Deep, Rock, Hell Below, and Hermit Caves. Burnet Cave is located in the wall of an arroyo on the east side of the mountains, 33 miles west of Carlsbad. It was excavated in 1931. Under the uppermost 3 feet of Basketmaker debris were Folsom points together with bones of bison and musk ox. Horse and camel bones also occurred under the Basketmaker layer. Pueblo and Mogollon remains have been found in the foothills. Thus, the area was evidently inhabited off and on by man since Pleistocene times. Apache Indians occupied the Guadalupe Mountains until the last century. From there they raided the settlements and retreated into the rugged canyons when pursued. After the coming of the Americans, bandits and outlaws used the limestone caves near the Butterfield Trail as hideouts, and it is said that more stagecoaches were held up in this vicinity than anywhere else on the trail. Captain Pat Garret was finally called in to get rid of the thieves, rustlers, and murderers who had collected there.

Only a portion of the Guadalupe Mountains is wooded. Wild Turkeys were exterminated in 1907 and replanted during the years of 1928-31. Deer, elk, black bear, coyote, and mountain lion now live in the National Forest.

The east and south sides of the mountains (on Texas Hill, Bandanna Point, El Paso Gap, and Carlsbad Caverns West quads) have numerous canyons. Among these are: Dark Canyon which has Indian paintings, Last Chance and Sitting Bull Canyons with Sitting Bull Falls and a picnic ground, Big Canyon (the start of the Golden Stairway trail), and others. The east side of the range is served by State Road 137 from U.S. 285, 12 miles north of Carlsbad, and primitive roads from Hope on State Road 82. Continuing south and west on State Road 137 one can drive to the top of the rim. This road leads northwest along the entire ridge and connects with the secondary roads from Hope.

The fire lookout on top of the ridge on the south side of Dark Canyon (Dark Canyon Lookout) at 6,950' can be reached by jeep. The Sitting Bull Falls (4,600') are 44 miles from Carlsbad, 8 miles on a side road from the end of the blacktop; the Sitting Bull Falls picnic ground is below the falls. Various trails make other canyons, ridges, and caves accessible from these roads.

THE BROKEOFF MOUNTAINS

This range, on Texas Hill quad, is a small spur of the Guadalupe Mountains on the southwest side of the rim. It joins the main range south of the state line in Texas. The bare ridge is named Brokeoff Mountains. It is on public domain, rises to an elevation of 5,900', and is used mainly for sheep grazing.

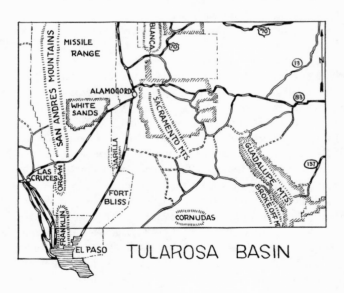

THE CORNUDAS MOUNTAINS

The Cornudas (horned) Mountains consist of a number of hills along the New Mexico-Texas line in Otero County, halfway between El Paso and Carlsbad Caverns. They include Cornudas Mountain (5,730'), Wind Mountain (7,280'), and Alamo Mountain (6,670'), on Alamo Mountain quad. Near the old Pine Springs Station on the Butterfield Trail on the southern side of the mountains there are thousands of petroglyphs and blackened caves with remnants of plaster. Boulders and cliffs are literally covered with petroglyphs and the caves with red paintings. Abundant Basketmaker remains have been found on the east side of the mountains and in the Hueco Hills west of the Cornudas. Black and white Salinas pottery found there was dated about 800 years ago. In the 19th century these mountains were one of the many Apache hideouts.

THE JARILLA MOUNTAINS

The Jarilla Mountains are north of Orogrande (much gold) on U.S. 54 between Alamogordo and El Paso. The low north-south range is approximately 8 miles long and 3 miles wide and is composed chiefly of monzonite porphyry and carboniferous limestone. The isolated peaks with their deep canyons were used by Geronimo as a stronghold.

Turquoise mining in the mountains dates back to the prehistoric Indians, as evidenced by stone tools, pottery, metatas, and manos, which were found nearby. Apache Indians and Spaniards continued the operation. Americans began prospecting the Jarillas in 1879 and found extensive iron and copper veins along with gold, silver, and turquoise deposits. During the gold rush of 1906-14 there were 2,000 residents in Orogrande. Iron ore consisting of hematite and magnetite was shipped to Pueblo, Colorado, from 1916 to 1921. The gold, silver, copper, and lead ores which were mined from 1904 until 1929 are valued at 1.5 million dollars.

The mountains are divided by a low pass, Monte Carlo Gap (4,232'). The northern section has a summit 4,851' high and the southern section has three peaks with 5,301', 5,210', and 4,851' elevations. The mountains are now in the White Sands Missile Range.

THE FRANKLIN MOUNTAINS

The greater part of the Franklin Mountains is located in the State of Texas. The section extending north into New Mexico, on Anthony quad, has one summit, North Anthonys Nose (5,368'), a low pass, Anthony Gap (4,424') on the south side near the state line, and Webb Gap on the northern end. The mountain is on state land and of little interest to mountaineers. It is east of Highways 80 and 85 between El Paso and Las Cruces and in full view of the road.

BISHOP CAP

Bishop Cap (5,419'), on Bishop Cap quad, 15 miles southeast of Las Cruces and east of the highway to El Paso is the highest of a series of north-south ridges. These are fault blocks similar to the Franklin Mountains and composed of Ordovician and Pennsylvanian sediments. Veins of fluorite and barite occur on the southwest side.

Conkling's Cave on the west side of the ridge was excavated in 1929. It contained bones of man, together with those of extinct sloths, cave bears, camels, bisons, horses, and dire wolves, but no artifacts.

THE POTRILLO MOUNTAINS

A group of hills between Columbus and El Paso is designated as East and West Potrillo Mountains (on Mt. Riley and Aden quads). The East Potrillo Range is a small narrow mountain ridge with a maximum elevation of 5,359'. A separate dome-shaped uplift on the northwest side is named Mount Riley (5,915') and west of this mountain are a large number of small hills extending nearly 30 miles from U.S 70-80 to the Mexican border, the highest of which is 5,408'. The only one of these hills named on the U. S. G. S. maps is Guzman's Lookout Mountain (4,762').

THE FLORIDA MOUNTAINS

The Florida Mountains, on Deming quad, were named by the Spaniards because of the flora in their parks. The north-south range is located on public domain southeast of Deming. A low hogback on the east side is called Little Florida Mountains. It contained one of the largest manganese-iron deposits which was mined for many years.

A few small caves in the Florida Mountains contained evidence of prehistoric occupation. In later times these mountains were Apache territory, lying on the Apache Trail between the Black Range and the Sierra Madre Mountains in Mexico. The Apache chief Victorio was wounded near Bear Springs in an encounter with prospectors from Pinos Altos who were looking for rich float in the mountains. The Apache were scattered by troops from Fort Cummings and Victorio died at Palomas Lake in the Sierra Madres.

The north side of the Florida Mountains has low ridges and brushy hogbacks while the south side has steep drops and sharp ridges. The main ridge has several summits over 7,000' high. When seen from a distance, the mountains have a striking silhouette which has been likened to a battleship. At one time there was more vegetation on the ridges and there were said to be many mountain goats. Now there are only a few black-tail deer. Some goat ranches are located in the hills.

Low grade lead-zinc ores have been mined in the past, and small veins of gold and silver have been found in the granite on the west side, but there is no mining at present. A considerable part of the range consists of volcanic rocks.

THE TRES HERMANAS MOUNTAINS

The Tres Hermanas (Three Sisters) Mountains, on Columbus quad, west of Columbus are low mountains with a north-south trend. They are divided into northern and southern sections by a secondary road which crosses the divide at 4,801′. The highest point in the northern part is 5,801′ high and there were trails in the valleys of this section in 1917. The southern mountains reach an elevation of 5,229′. Gold, silver, and copper deposits in the mountains have been mined in the past. A cave on the eastern slope of the mountains has spectacular fluorescent minerals.

SOUTHWESTERN
NEW MEXICO

THE VICTORIO MOUNTAINS

These mountains are a geologically complex group of low hills, 16 miles west of Deming and just south of Highway 70-80. The highest point is 5,260′ and the hills rise about 700′ above the plains.

THE LITTLE HATCHET MOUNTAINS

The Little Hatchet Mountains, on Hachita quad, are a small north-south range 6 miles west of Hachita (Spanish, little hatchet). Turquoise was mined in these mountains in prehistoric times. Stone hammers and other artifacts were found in the ancient workings. The deposits were rediscovered in 1878 and operated since 1885 intermittently for about 25 years. Numerous mines in the vicinity of Old Hachita and Turquoise Mountain on the north side of the range (Eureka district) have furnished good quality turquoise.

THE BIG HATCHET MOUNTAINS

These mountains south of the Little Hatchet Mountains, on Big Hatchet Peak quad, rise to an elevation of 8,366′ at Hatchet Peak. The mountains are separated from the Little Hatchet Mountains by Hatchet Gap (4,318′) through which State Road 81 from Hachita goes. They contain galena, gypsum, malachite, smithsonite, and sphalerite.

THE SIERRA RICA

Sierra Rica, northeast of the Big Hatchet Mountains, is a very small range with a maximum elevation of 5,495'.

THE CEDAR MOUNTAIN RANGE

The mountains east of Hachita, on Victorio quad, are known as Cedar Mountain Range, or sometimes as Hachita Mountains. In the 1880s this area was cattle country with plentiful grass. Hundreds of antelope and many birds were seen. During several years of drought nearly all vegetation was killed. Heavy rains washed down the bushes and filled the canyons with debris, so that the mountains were hardly recognizable. A renegade Indian, the Apache Kid (Zenogalache, The Crazy One), raided this region. He was educated in Carlisle, Pennsylvania, and could speak Spanish and English. After many mysterious killings, stockmen tracked him to the San Mateos at the head of Kelly Canyon in 1905. He is buried at the spot where he was killed. Named summits in the Cedar Mountain Range are Cedar Mountain (6,207') and Flying W Mountain (6,217'), the highest point in the range.

THE PYRAMID MOUNTAINS

The Pyramid Mountains directly south of Lordsburg, on Lordsburg quad, are a north-south fault block 22 miles long and 3-7 miles wide. They have been mined for copper, gold, silver, lead, and zinc, which occur in veins. The ghost towns Shakespeare and Valedon, 2 miles southwest of Lordsburg, are in the center of the old mining district at the foot of Lookout Hill and 85 Hill (5,105'). A tramway hauled ore from the mines near Lee Peak (5,022') to Shakespeare. Other mines were farther south in a canyon west of Aberdeen Peak (5,044'). The mines yielded an estimated 25 million dollars' worth of ore.

The Pyramid Mountains consist of basalt overlain by Miocene rhyolytic volcanics. The two major summits, North Pyramid Peak (6,002') and South Pyramid Peak (5,910') are volcanic necks. Other summits are: Rimrock Mountain (5,785'), Niggerhead (4,993'), Swallow Fork Peak (4,954'), Dogs Head (4,812'), Cedar Knob (4,902), Goat Mountain (5,607'), Kirk Peak (5,359'), and Lightning Dock Mountain. The Leitendorf Mine is just north of the Leitendorf Hills west of North Pyramid Peak, which rise to an elevation of 5,338'.

THE ANIMAS MOUNTAINS

The Animas Mountains form the east side of the Animas Valley in the southwestern corner of New Mexico. They consist of Mezozoic and Tertiary formations and rise to an altitude of 8,519′ at Animas Peak, on Animas Peak quad. State Road 79 crosses the mountains near the Mexican border at San Luis Pass (5,522′), separating a small group of hills south of the pass which is referred to as San Luis Mountains (6,751′). The southern tip of the main range culminates in Hilo Peak (5,955′). The low hills south of State Road 79 are called Whitewater Mountains. The continental divide runs along the entire ridge of the Animas and San Luis Mountains and crosses the Mexican border. In 1918 a secondary road traversed Playas Lake and the northern part of the range at Whitmire Pass (4,992′), on Playas quad.

THE PELONCILLO MOUNTAINS

These mountains are a narrow range of low hills rising 1,000-1,500' above the Animas and San Simon Valleys on both sides of the New Mexico-Arizona border. They are composed of Tertiary volcanic rocks. The southern section is in Coronado National Forest and appears on Cienega Springs and Animas Peak quads. The mountains are crossed by U.S. 70-80 at Steins Pass (4,350'), a former station on the Butterfield Stage Line to California; by U.S. 80 south of Road Forks; by State Road 9 at Antelope Pass (5,574'); and by State Road 79 in the southwest corner of New Mexico. Other passes are Granite Gap (4,460'), Guadalupe Pass, and Cowboy Pass.

Peaks in the southern part of the range are: Black Point (6,467'), Bunk Robinson Peak (6,241'), Guadalupe Mountain (6,450'), Black Mountain, and Mount Baldy. A few hills in the southern extremity of the range are designated as Guadalupe Mountains on Cienega Springs quad.

ROCK CLIMBING
(with contributions from Ernest C. Anderson)

All major peaks in New Mexico can be climbed by routes which involve little or no difficulties beyond what an average climber in good condition can do. There are, however, smaller mountains, cliffs, and towers, and certain climbing routes which offer a challenge even to skilled climbers. Among these are the Organ Mountains, the Brazos Cliffs, Shiprock, and other volcanic necks, and a number of faces and ridges in the Sangre de Cristo and Sandia Mountains. Brief descriptions of some of these routes are given for the benefit of experienced mountaineers. They are not intended as complete guides for these routes, which would require far more detailed directions, but rather as a listing of climbing areas and routes.

Safe climbing on any of these routes requires the teamwork of roped parties with a thorough knowledge of belaying techniques and other safe climbing practices, conditioning, and above all, experience. It is emphasized that on any such rock climbing expedition hard hats are essential. Loose rock is everywhere. In recent years the mountaineering clubs have started offering climbing schools, usually at nominal cost, to teach safe climbing, and it is hoped that all beginners will avail themselves of such opportunities to gain experience and technical knowledge safely. Mountain climbing clubs in Albuquerque, Las Cruces, and Los Alamos now offer climbing schools. Suggested reading on this subject is **Mountaineering, the Freedom of the Hills** by the Climbing Committee of the Seattle Mountaineers and **Basic Rockcraft** by Royal Robbins, La Siesta Press, 1971, Glendale, California. **Summit Magazine** is a continuing source of up-to-date information on techniques and routes.

The classification of climbing routes used in this chapter has been taken from **Mountaineering, the Freedom of the Hills** and is quoted, as follows:

Class 1:   Walking; shoes helpful.

2:    Scrambling, using hands; boots desirable.

3:    Easy climbing, somewhat exposed; rope should be worn.

4:    Moderate climbing, very exposed; belaying essential.

5:    Difficult climbing, very exposed; pitons or other anchors used to protect the leader.

6:    Extremely difficult climbing; pitons or other equipment used as direct aid.

Most of the spectacular cliffs and faces in New Mexico have been climbed at this writing. In addition to the areas mentioned below, Cleopatras Needle and Venus Needle in Todilto Park and the precipitous faces on Hermit Peak have been scaled.

Shiprock (7,178'), one of the most famous landmarks in New Mexico, is a sheer volcanic plug of unprecedented size. It is composed predominantly of grey-brown welded tuff (volcanic ash) with intrusions of dark basalt and rises some 1,700' above the desert floor, approximately 10 miles west of the town of Shiprock on the northern edge of the Navajo Reservation. To the Navajo, it was Tsae-bidahi (Rock with Wings) and according to one legend represents the great bird which brought them from the north.

Although various attempts were made to climb Shiprock in the thirties, it remained unclimbed until 1939. In 1937, a Colorado Mountain Club party led by R. M. Ormes made several all-out attacks on the mountain but failed to find the key gully which led down (not up) to the traverse around the North Summit (the Minor Spire of the drawing.) Four Sierra Club members (B. Robinson, R. Bedayn, J. Dyer and D. Brower) found the solution and reached the summit on 12 October, 1939, after 4 days' climbing. The second ascent of what was once called America's toughest mountain was made twelve and one-half years later by 5 members of the Colorado Mountain Club led by Dale Johnson. Since then Shiprock has been climbed over a hundred times.

Unfortunately, climbing of this beautiful spire, and indeed of all monoliths on the reservation, has been strictly forbidden by the

Navajos and the prohibition is being energetically enforced. The ban originated in the spring of 1970 following an accident on the rock occasioned by a sudden Easter snow squall. It was formalized in 1971 by Charles Damon (Director of Navajo Parks and Recreation, Window Rock, Navajo Nation (Arizona), 86515) to whom requests or remonstrances should be directed. The reasons advanced for the prohibition are "the nature of the rocks themselves, which cannot stand unnecessary attrition" (perhaps true of Totem Pole and Spider Rock but hardly of Shiprock) and "the monoliths of the Navajo Reservation are considered sacred places. To climb them is to profane them." The Navajos plan severe penalties (directed toward the pocketbook rather than the scalp) for persons violating the ban. In view of this situation, climbers are advised to stay away from the reservation until such time as permission is officially available. In the meantime, the following brief account of routes on the rock is given as a matter of historical interest. More detailed route descriptions can be found in a number of fine articles in *Summit* magazine.

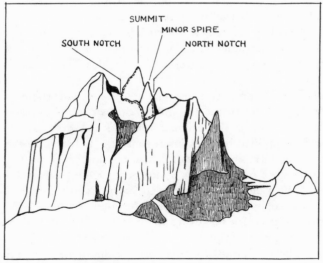

SHIPROCK EAST FACE

Shiprock pinnacle is reached easily by ordinary cars from either the north or the south, but drivers are warned of high centers and wash-outs on both routes. In addition, a sudden rain storm can make the ground very greasy and slippery. In these respects, the southern approach is more reliable. Follow U.S. 666 south from the town of Shiprock about 8 miles beyond the junction with State Road 504 to the Red Rock highway. Go west on this "highway" until it passes through the Great South Dike of Shiprock. Turn north on a primitive track just east of the dike. Near the base of the rock, another track (the desert is full of them) turns west and passes over the dike. Immediately beyond, a very primitive trace leads to the usual camp site at the foot of the magnificent west wall. Fred Beckey, who made the first ascent of this side of the rock in 1965 said "Never had I been able to get a car so close to the beginning of a major climb."

The alternate route to the rock from the north is now well-marked by signs reading "Pinnacle" and is somewhat shorter. It turns south from State Road 504 about five miles west of the junction with U.S. 666 and approaches the rock from the east. Several short roads lead up to the foot of the talus on the east and south. Overnight camping at the rock is now forbidden; the nearest legal site is at the junction of U.S. 666 and the Red Rock highway where there are a pair of covered picnic tables. There are no trees or water at any of these spots.

While there are three extremely difficult aid routes on the southwest and east faces, the only route available to the average advanced climber is the original route of the first ascent party, somewhat simplified by later improvements. It begins in the Black Bowl, a huge intrusion of basalt lava at the northwest corner. Here six pitches (one of them class 5) lead up the steep but well-broken blocks to the Colorado Col (labeled North Notch in the illustration). This col lies at the boundary between the black basalt and the brown tuff which makes up the major portion of the monolith and which gives Shiprock its characteristic smooth, rounded texture. The south wall of this col is the flank of the North Summit or Fin (labeled Minor Spire in the illustration). Projecting from

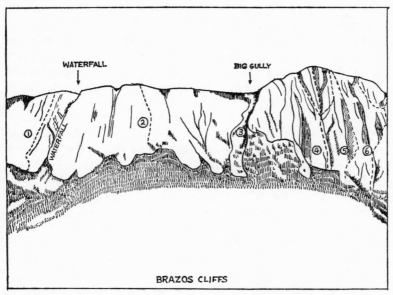

WATERFALL   BIG GULLY

WATERFALL

BRAZOS CLIFFS

its surface is Ormes Rib, a very unreliable dike which has been climbed several times but which is *not* a route to the Main Summit. The key is the *descent* of the Rappel Gully which leads down to the eastern base of the North Summit. Two ropes must be left behind at these rappels and must be prusiked on the return. The route is now on the southeast side of the rock where a very thin and exposed friction traverse leads around the obstacle and into the Honeycomb Gully. Another fixed rope is usually left on this traverse which could be rendered impassable by a sudden storm.

The famous double overhangs of the early climbs are now bypassed by an extremely exposed but well-protected step-around to the left which gives access to the Upper Honeycomb Gully and some welcome scrambling. (On the descent, a rappel is made down the double overhangs at the top of which are two fine, if shallow, bivouac caves.)

The scramble up the gully (really a large bowl at this point) is interrupted by one class 4 pitch: the ramp, an easy friction walk-up when dry, but exposed and hence dangerous when wet. Above this, it is an easy scramble to the South Col (or Notch) in the shadow of the Horn, the crux pitch of the climb. This pitch has been climbed free by a very few climbers but is usually done with aid (three stirrups.) The final move up the Horn requires the climber to emerge on very thin holds onto the west side of the rock above the appalling west wall, 1200 feet of near-vertical slabs. Fortunately for the acrophobic leader, it is possible to throw a rope over the Horn so that an upper belay is available. Above the Horn, one aid and two free pitches lead directly up the southeast side of the summit spire.

Descent follows virtually the route of the ascent (and takes almost as long) but with generous use of rappels, which permit by-passing a few of the more devious pitches. At the Colorado Col but farther to the west and somewhat below the point of entry, an excellent anchor of two firm bolts permits a two-rope, partly free rappel avoiding the long diagonal route used up the headwall of the Black Bowl.

An alternate beginning, used first on the third ascent by Bill Long and Bob Skinner (in 1952) is more elegant in that it avoids the easy, fractured basalt of the Black Bowl and stays in the smooth tuff which is the essence of the rock. It follows Long's Couloir which begins just to the right (south) of the basalt intrusion and circles the north side of the great northwest buttress of the Main Summit. The rim of the Black Bowl is reached from the opposite (south) side after a very thin ascent of an ever-steepening, parabolic headwall. The minute saddle of tuff joining the west wall of the fin with the basalt of the bowl at this point is called the Sierra Col since the first ascent party reached here from the north. A short but difficult and exposed move up blocks of basalt projecting from the tuff leads into the fixed rappel point just below the Colorado Col where this variant joins the normal route.

Virtually the entire route can be seen from below but the observer must make a complete circuit of the rock starting on the northwest side for the beginning, hurrying to the southeast for the Traverse and Honeycomb Gully, and then to the west for the crux pitch at the Horn. Fortunately the circumference of the rock (about a mile) permits this easily.

While the ascent has been made in as little as 7 hours (round trip) by strong parties familiar with the route, many parties bivouac on the rock. Ascents have been made in every month of the year but the weather is cold and unreliable in winter and spring, excruciatingly hot in summer. October is the month of choice. Shiprock is still a difficult climb and considerable caution and advance planning are advisable. There have been two fatalities, both due to rappel failures during the descent.

The Brazos Cliffs. These sheer cliffs of Precambrian quartzite are a prodigious fault scarp dating from some 70 million years ago. They are located in northern New Mexico only 17 miles south of the Colorado line and mark an abrupt boundary between the 7500' farming and grazing lands along the Rio Chama and the 10,000' rolling plateau of the Brazos high country. (See the Brazos Peak and Cebolla USGS quads.) The area is entirely privately

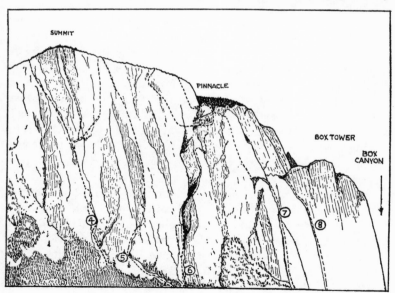

owned and access is therefore limited. To reach the region drive 70 miles north from Espanola on U.S. 84 past Tierra Amarilla. Shortly after crossing the Rio Brazos, turn right (east) on N.M. 512 and drive 7.5 miles to Brazos Lodge (7,950′). Permission to continue to the Main Cliffs (El Ventisquero Amarillo) which lie directly ahead should be sought here from the management. It is best to leave cars at the Lodge and hike into the cliffs (about an hour's walk.)

The cliffs north of the river face southwest and hence remain in shadow until midmorning. The rock is generally excellent; the quartzite has a good "tooth" and provides excellent traction when dry, but frequent lichens are treacherously slippery when wet. The quartzite is inherently of a reddish hue, but the lichens tint it green, yellow, or grey. The appearance of the red usually signals overhang or recent rockfall, either of which suggests the route lies elsewhere. Climbing holds and piton cracks are numerous and tree-anchors are frequent. The quartzite is so hard that it is impossible to set bolts, but they are never required.

The cliffs are divided into two sections by the Big Gully normally used as the descent route (Route 3), a class 2 scramble which is too difficult to be a walk but too easy to be a climb. A "trail" is slowly developing close to the cliffs on its southeast side. To the northwest of the gully the cliffs are lower and the rock, in general less reliable. Just above the Brazos Lodge there appears briefly during the height of the spring run-off a very spectacular waterfall. Route 1 is one of several Waterfall rib routes (class 3 to 4) which increase in difficulty from west to east. The Notch Route (Route 2) is named for the prominent square gap on the ridge just west of the Big Gully.

The best and longest routes (medium class 5) are found to the right of the Big Gully. Route 4, the Great Couloir, has 17 pitches by the direct finish and leads to the highest point of the wall in a spectacularly exposed climax. About halfway up, two easier alternatives branch off. The normal finish stays left in the Great Couloir proper while the Escape Route follows wide, tree-covered ledges in a long scramble to join Easy Ridge to the right. The first five pitches, which are common to the three variants, are in a dark gully and can be dangerous from snow and ice fall in early season.

Route 5, the so-called Easy Ridge, is a beautiful, exposed route up the crest of an arete of a sound but well-broken rock. The usual route has 13 pitches, but 5 more can be added at the bottom by beginning at the lowest point of the talus rather than scrambling 400 feet up the gully to the left. The last third of the way to the top is a relatively easy scramble.

Route 6 is called "Going to Jerusalem" because of its devious nature. It is long, but the difficulties are not sustained and there is much scrambling between the two crux pitches (the first and the last). It begins in Jerusalem Gully and when this steepens into a headwall it traverses to Pinnacle Gully. There are a number of variant endings. Additional routes to the Pinnacle begin farther east.

Numerous other routes covering a range of difficulty have been put up on the Ventisquero—in fact few major lines have not been climbed—but a detailed enumeration would be out of place here.

All of the routes lead to the summit (10,701') from which a half-mile hike east leads to the edge of the Brazos Box Canyon with magnificent views down into a superb, rugged gorge nearly half a mile deep. The return is best made by skirting the bottom of the talus slope on the north side of the Summit and contouring into Big Gully. The descent is somewhat easier close to the cliffs on their east side.

Access to the Box Canyon of the Brazos is blocked by the private land of Corkin's Lodge. Transit is limited to guests of this exclusive lodge which caters primarily to fishermen. Climbers can however reach the box by taking to the cliffs outside Corkin's fences. Since the Rio Brazos fills the canyon literally wall-to-wall in many places, access is impossible during spring flood and difficult at all times. The stream can be waded during the summer with due regard for its great variability of depth and current and its slippery rocks. The crystal clarity of the water makes navigation easy. A number of very difficult climbs on the north wall of the box have been reported in **American Alpine Journal.**

Another set of equally spectacular cliffs, called the "Encinado Wedge," continues south of the Rio Brazos in the triangle between Box Canyon and Encinado Creek. They, too, are entirely on private land and the only access to their base is by a primitive jeep road which follows the historic route of the Tierra Amarilla-Tres Piedras stage line. A number of difficult class 5 routes have recently been put up the major ridges of this face.

A new road is currently being developed from Tierra Amarilla across the high plateau to Tres Piedras. It will eventually be part of an extended U.S. 64 running entirely across northern New Mexico. The present designation is State Road 111 west from Tres Piedras and State Road 553 east from Tierra Amarilla. Most of it exists as an excellent graveled road and it provides another potential route to the beauties of the Brazos Box, this time from above, but with the same limitation: private land. One turns east from U.S. 84 onto State Road 553 about 1.5 miles south of Tierra Amarilla. A 20-mile drive on good road leads to the plateau (10,400') with the cliffs some 3 miles away to the northwest. If the owner grants permission, which he hesitates to do during the summer grazing season, it is easy to stroll across rolling pasture land to the brink of the Encinado Wedge and to some fantastic views down into the Box Canyon. Best time is in October when the aspen are at their golden prime.

Brazos Peak (11,288'), the highest summit on the Brazos Peak quad, is on private land (Tierra Amarilla Grant). It is some 4 miles north of the Brazos Box and may be reached on foot from the top of the cliffs, e.g., via Route 3. Permission is required to use any of the jeep roads north of the Brazos Cliffs.

Cabezon (Spanish, big head) (8,000'), on Cabezon Peak quad, is the largest of a number of volcanic necks in the Rio Puerco valley south of Cuba. Its sheer sides rise nearly 2,000' above the valley floor. To the Navajo Indians it is a sacred mountain. There is still a shrine on its summit which has been visited within recent times. The mountain is called also Tse Najin (black rock) and by legend is the head of the giant Ye-itso who was killed by the Twin War Brothers on Mount Taylor.

To reach Cabezon drive 20 miles north from San Ysidro on State Road 44 and turn left on an unmarked dirt road. This road goes west and southwest 9 miles to San Luis and 5 miles beyond to the ghost town of Cabezon, which is just east of the road. One can continue a short distance past Cabezon on the top of a low mesa to a point near the south edge of the mountain. A short hike east from the road leads to the base of the cliffs. Cabezon has been climbed from the west side along a sloping ridge which meets the face some 50' below the top. The upper part of this route is very exposed and has loose rock hazard.

The preferred class 3 climbing route is on the southeast side. It starts in a partially hidden gully. Near the top of this gully, where it becomes vertical, traverse left (south) on firm basalt blocks to an easy slope which leads to the upper cliffs. A shallow notch in the rim is reached by staying slightly to the left of the center. From there one can walk to the top. There is some exposure on the rocks and inexperienced groups may wish to rope on.

The Dona Ana Mountains (from information by R. Ingraham). This small mountain range is north of Las Cruces and east of U.S. 85 and is reached from the Jornada del Muerto Road. Turn off left from U.S. 70, about 6 miles north of Las Cruces and drive north until the main group of the Doña Anas is directly west. There are 4 summits in this group. A huge 4-500' rock wall is visible on the east side of the nearest summit. This face is grooved at regular intervals, giving the effect of a huge checkerboard. It was first climbed by Ingraham and Anuta in 1964.

A good side road leads to the north side of the main peaks. Turn west from the Jornada del Muerto Road just before reaching two stone gate towers on this road, and leave cars on the north side of the mountains. From there the south edge of the great face is reached in an hour's walk. The face is traversed diagonally to the north side on class 4 ledges, crossing the great central groove which is near vertical. The route traverses back into the face and heads for the summit, which is estimated to be 5,800'. The highest summit is Doña Ana Peak (5,899'). The other summits in the group are easily accessible from the same parking area.

Early occupation of this region is indicated by petroglyphs on the lower cliffs and the finding of artifacts, including pottery, near the small mountains just north of the Doña Anas.

Climbing Routes in the Sandia Mountains
(from information by George Bell)

The Knife Edge is on the ridge which runs northwest from Sandia Peak and forms the north rim of Juan Tabo Canyon. It offers a spectacular rock climb (class 4) on sound granite. The trail to the ridge starts from the extreme northeast curve of the road beyond Juan Tabo picnic ground and goes north to the wooded crest. To gain the ridge nearer the rocks, leave the trail below the crest and traverse east (right). The ridge crest to the southeast starts as a walk. It becomes progressively more rocky and exposed until the top of a shoulder is reached where the spectacular Knife Edge comes into view. This exposed section requires three or four leads of roped climbing. A few pitons may be found desirable. In spite of its steepness, however, the ridge offers few technical difficulties to qualified climbers. It may serve as a warning that there have been two fatalities on this ridge. If the descent is made by the Knife Edge, a single 100′ rappel at the top is the easiest way down. The return trip can be made via the La Luz trail, but the bushy Juan Tabo Canyon is not recommended.

The Shield is the steep south face of the Knife Edge. It offers several climbing routes of 1,000′ or more. A route that is a class 5 starts from a grove of trees which extends well into the center of the Shield. From the trees, climb gradually east (right) into the broken face until it steepens a few hundred feet below the top. The face is then traversed left 200′ on a ledge (which narrows at the end) to a gully ascending diagonally up to the east (right). From the right head of this gully a steep 100′ pitch leads directly to the ridge a few hundred feet above the Knife Edge.

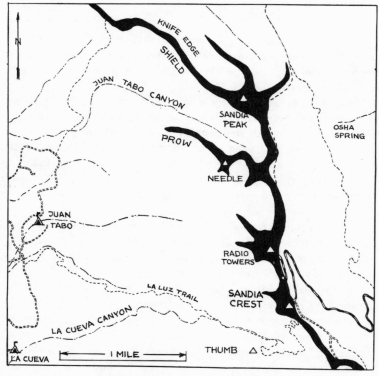

SANDIA PEAK REGION

The Needle is a rock standing in front of the rim north of Sandia Crest. It is usually climbed from the top of the scarp by dropping to a saddle and from there by the southeast ridge to the summit.

The Prow, a small face with class 3 routes, is located below the Needle. It can be reached easily from the Juan Tabo Recreation Area and is used for practice climbing.

For more information on the Sandias, technical climbers should refer to **Guide to the Sandia Mountains** edited by L. G. Kline.

The Organ Mountains

These mountains form the eastern skyline of the city of Las Cruces. The range consists of an amazing number of spires and pinnacles which lie on the 20-mile ridge between San Augustin Peak at the north end and Rattlesnake Ridge east of the village of Mesquite. On old maps these mountains are named "La Sierra de la Soledad" (Spanish, Mountains of Solitude), and they are that, even now, despite the proximity of a fairly large city.

Geologically the range is an elongated fault block, uplifted highest on the east. The center is a tertiary monzonite batholith carved into jagged needles which resemble organ pipes. The lower elevations have more recent Paleozoic sedimentary rocks, overlain by Tertiary volcanic deposits.

The mountains rise almost 5,000' from the valley floor and have considerable brush cover on the slopes and in the gullies up to the summits. White thorn, cholla, and yucca line the dim trails, and the loose rocks provide cover for the rattlesnakes. U.S. 70 crosses the Organ Mountains at San Augustin Pass and furnishes access to the northern section of the mountains. Most of the mining activity was centered around this region. Lead and silver were first discovered in 1849. Mining started in 1854 in spite of the Apache and reached boom proportions during 1881-1906. The village of Organ just west of the pass was the largest mining camp near the old Torpedo mine which produced copper in 1907. The tailings are just above the camp. The organ district has yielded some 2.5 million dollars' worth of copper, lead, silver, gold, and zinc ores. The mining activities diminished by 1912 but some mining continues to the present day.

In 1867, a hermit named Giovanni Maria de Augustino, who came from the Las Vegas region, settled in a cave in the Organ Mountains. Only a short time later he was found dead with an Apache lance through his heart.

When the Wheeler survey expedition came through this region in the 1870's, they described the Organs as "lofty, rugged, and inaccessible." The first recorded ascent of the highest summit, the

Organ Needle, was made in 1904 by W. I. Isaacks and O. B. Metcalfe at the request of their professor at the A and M College in Las Cruces who wanted a flag on the summit. They raised a pole with some kind of flag, which remained there for many years. Sugarloaf was climbed by a local party in the 30's and the south Rabbit Ear, probably earlier. Local people also climbed easy summits, such as Organ Peak. The German "paper-clip" scientists, who were brought to White Sands Proving Ground in 1946-47, climbed some of the steeper walls.

Little was heard about climbing in the Organs until Warren Gorrell, Jr., published his account of the climb of the Wedge in 1954. On top of the Wedge he found a note from S. H. Christensen who climbed the mountain in 1934 and another from McCord, Burwell, and Vickers, who made the ascent in 1950. These original entries were still on the mountain in 1964.

Intensive climbing, however, was undertaken only in the last 16 years when an active group of climbers of the Southwestern Mountaineers climbed every major peak by several routes. There are now over 100 separate climbing routes in the Organs and a "Guide to the Organ Mountains" is in preparation by Professor Richard Ingraham of Las Cruces.*

Climbing in the Organs is rather different from other mountains in New Mexico. It is necessary to carry water. One must learn to avoid the ever-present cactus, thornbush, and yucca, and climbers frequently clap hands to induce rattlesnakes to rattle so that they may be avoided. Loose rock hazard is present on most routes except in the Rabbit Ears, which have excellent solid rock. Once climbers have become used to these hazards which the Organs present, they seem to be drawn back irresistibly to this fascinating array of needles, towers, walls, and buttresses.

San Augustin Peak is accessible from the pass road U.S. Highway 70 as are Baylor Peaks and Baylor Pass (6,400′), named

---

*The author is indebted to Dick Ingraham for most of the information on the Organ routes, for his kind hospitality, and for an interesting climb of the Wedge.

for the Confederate general who went through the pass in 1861 to capture the Union troops under General Lynde at San Augustin Springs, 2 miles east of San Augustin Pass.

The Rabbit Ears and other peaks in the northern part of the Organs are reached from the Topp Hut, named in honor of Bernie Topp, who was fatally injured on a climb of Shiprock in 1956. The road to the hut turns off from U.S. Highway 70 at the settlement of Butterfield, southwest of San Augustin Pass, and runs south to the old Isaacks (now Cox) Ranch, south around the ranch, and east for a total of 5.4 miles. The road continues 0.6 miles to a fluorite mine (private).

Organ Needle, Organ Peak, Organ Baldy, and the High Horns are climbed from near Cuevas (Spanish, cave) Rock (5,816'), a yellow sandstone formation with a cave at the south side of the base. The cave contained evidence of early occupations in the form of skeletons and artifacts. One can drive to within 100 yards of Cuevas Rock by going 12.5 miles east from Las Cruces on University Avenue extension. The road goes around Tortugas Mountain (4,931'), on Tortugas Mountain quad, which still has a shrine of the Tortugas Indians on its top.

Much of the east side of the Organ Mountains is on the White Sands Missile Range and permission is required to enter. It is advisable to make local inquiries also about trails on the west side of the mountains as some of the trails run across private land (Cox Ranch) and Missile Range.

San Augustin Peak (7,025'), on Organ quad, at the northern tip of the Organ Mountains (or the south end of the San Augustin Mountains) is just north of San Augustin Pass (5,719') on U.S. 70 and overlooks the Organ mining district. It has a small rock cap, which looks unimpressive from the road. The mountain has been climbed from all sides by 13 different climbing routes. The start of any of these climbs can be reached in less than an hour from the highway. The east ridge is essentially a walk and can be climbed by the inexperienced. The summit offers fine views of the Organs, San Andres, and Sierra Blanca. The north face, which ordinarily is hidden from view, is a sheer wall of nearly

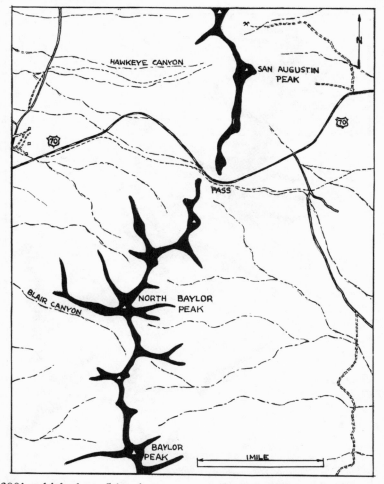

300′ which has 5th class routes with a challenge to expert climbers. The sloping south face has several 3rd class routes, while the southwest ridge is a short scramble. The west wall has one diagonal route and the sharp north-northwest ridge will go.

The Organ peaks south of Baylor Pass appear on Organ Peak quad. The access roads are described above.

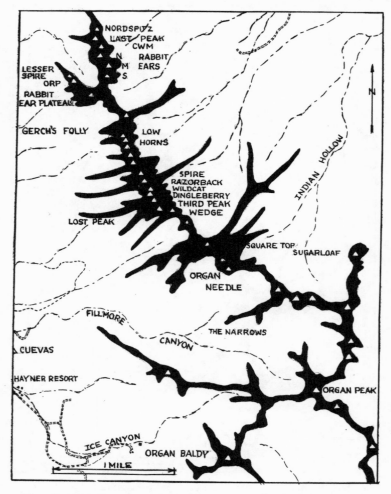

The Rabbit Ears are mountains with characteristic rounded tops and steep sides resembling rabbit ears, particularly from the northwest side. They are easily accessible from the mine above the Topp Hut, from where a short trail leads to Rabbit Ear Canyon. This canyon goes east and then southeast around a ridge with a series of needle-like prominences which culminate in a large summit called the Rabbit Ear Plateau. Starting at the low end of this ridge are the so-called Rabbit Ear Towers, the Lesser Spire, Orp, and, standing apart to the east, the Citadel. There are at present 9 routes on the North Rabbit Ear, the standard (easiest) route being "Boyer's Chute," a 3rd class route in the great chimney on the northwest face. The most difficult route is the north face via the "Awful Buttress." The Middle Rabbit Ear (8,150′) can be climbed by 5 difficult routes—there is no easy one. The normal route on the southeast side probably was climbed first by the German scientists. The smaller South Rabbit Ear has 4 routes, the standard route being on the northwest side.

Rabbit Ear Plateau (8,010′). This prominent peak southwest of the main Rabbit Ear group has a series of sharp west ridges, starting from the north, Rogowski's Rib, Long Rib, and Knife Rib. All of these named ridges have been climbed. Of particular interest is the climb of the south face and the Rabbit Ear Towers in the northwest ridge. The Citadel and the Lesser Spire are climbed usually by their north ridges. Orp has an unclimbed north face. The northeast ridge goes, but one must traverse into the north face near the top. The south side is an easy 3rd class climb.

The three small peaks north of the Rabbit Ears, Nordspitz, Last Peak, and Cwm, are also accessible from Rabbit Ear Canyon. Last Peak and Cwm are climbed from the west side and Nordspitz, by the Organ ridge route.

The central Organs or Organ Needles include the six Low Horns, the four High Horns, Third Peak, Lost Peak, and the Wedge. All six Low Horns normally are climbed via the Organ ridge routes. The buttress which forms the northwest extremity of the Low Horns has a 5th class route in its 800′ west face. It is called Gerch's Folly and can be reached by a short hike from the Topp Hut. The climb starts at the base of the great crack in the center of the face which is visible from the hut.

The Spire is the northernmost of the High Horns. The standard route in the north face starts from just below the saddle on the main ridge of the Organs between Low Horn No. 6 and the

Spire. Third class pitches lead up the base of the Spike, a 60'
gendarme visible from the west. All routes from this point require
rope. The standard route goes up alongside the Spike, traverses
into the north face, and heads straight up to the summit through
the "Obvious Gully." The other routes on the Spire are more
difficult.

Razorback, just south of the Spire, is somewhat higher. The
easy approach is the Organ ridge route from the south, the most
interesting route, the characteristic knife edge on the west side
(class 4 to 5). The Organ ridge route is used also for the two
next peaks south, Wildcat and Dingleberry (south approach).

Third Peak is climbed by the south face and Lost Peak by the
west ridge from well below the saddle between Wedge and Lost
Peak.

The Wedge (8,300') is the highest of the High Horns and
affords a magnificent view over the Organs. The normal route
from the north side of Cuevas Rock goes up an alluvial fan, and

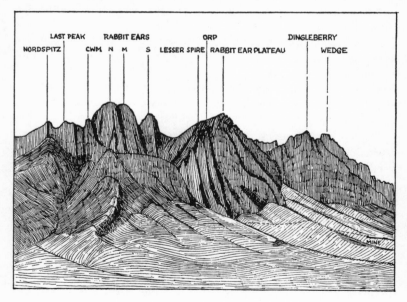

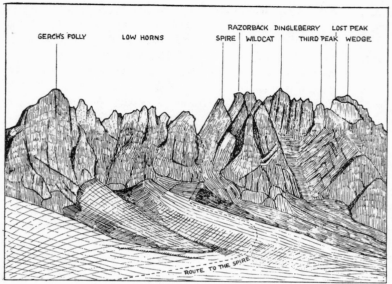

leads to the lowest saddle south of the peak. It is advisable to detour north from Cuevas about 100 yards around a section of Missile Range and Cox Ranch. From the saddle a sloping brushy ledge leads to the east side and a steep south-facing pitch to the northeast side of the summit pyramid. The summit is reached by a short climb on the northeast side. For the return trip one can descend west from the saddle between Lost Peak and Wedge, keeping right at two smaller saddles below. More difficult routes on the Wedge are the west ridge and the diagonal route in the southwest face.

The **Organ Needle** area is a high section of ridge with Squaretop (8,300'), Little Squaretop (8,919'), and the Needle (9,012'), the highest point in the Organs. Squaretop is normally climbed by the south ridge, Little Squaretop from the south side. The standard route on the Needle requires little climbing. It leads from Cuevas up Fillmore Canyon, then east toward the prominent "Yellow Rocks." Several hundred yards up the gully past these rocks one leaves the gully and heads up the slope to the right, following a relatively clear arroyo to the base of the "Grey Eminence," a prominent low western shoulder composed of crumbly volcanic rock. The route follows along the base of this rock to the saddle at its top which has several large junipers. The climb continues up the west side of the Needle through brush, following arroyos whenever possible. A small wall is climbed on its right side.

At the base of the summit tower the route goes up Dark Canyon on the right, a narrow canyon full of brush, flanked on the left by the summit tower and on the right by a prominent narrow wall. If one turns right too soon, this wall bars access to the summit. The rocks on the left at the top of Dark Canyon can be climbed to an easy 3rd class gully which leads to the top on the southwest side of the peak. As an alternate route one can continue past the little saddle in Dark Canyon some 50 yards down the other side and climb to the summit over even easier rock on

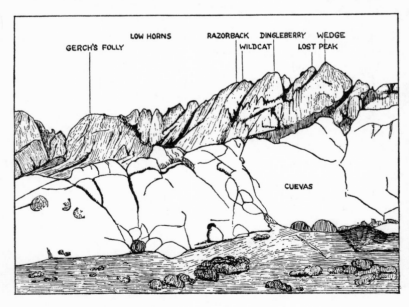

the south side. The same route is used ordinarily for the descent. The route is mostly 2nd class but for the final 3rd class pitch some may want rope. The normal time for the climb is 4-4.5 hours. Since Fillmore Canyon lies on the Fort Bliss Reservation and is partly on land leased by A. B. Cox, permission may be required for crossing it. Among the remaining 5 climbing routes on the Needle, the west wall is recommended.

Sugarloaf is a peculiar smooth rounded dome of firm whitish rock which is on a spur about a mile east from the main Organ ridge. The mountain can be approached either from the Missile Range or from the west side through Fillmore Canyon, the main ridge of the Organs, and farther on ridges to the base of the peak. The easy route starts on the east side and finishes in the north face of the mountain. A 5th class climbing route has been pioneered in the 1,000′ north face which is tilted at 45° or more. For the descent one normally rappels off the east side from a fixed piton to a lower platform from where another short rappel takes one to a saddle.

The **Organ Peak** (8,870′) is best climbed via the western approach to Sugarloaf. The route from Cuevas goes up Fillmore Canyon to the second canyon on the left (after about an hour's hike). It passes through the Narrows, a narrow pass between high and overhanging walls of friable rock, and follows the stream bed into a large bushy amphitheater. Climb northeast through the bush to the main ridge of the Organs, where Sugarloaf becomes visible, and continue east on the ridge to the junction with the Sugarloaf ridge. From there follow the ridge to the summit of Organ Peak. One can return the same way or drop directly from the peak into Fillmore Canyon. This is a 2nd class route requiring about 4-5 hours from Cuevas.

Organ Baldy (8,445′) can be climbed from the end of the road in Ice Canyon, which can be reached by continuing on the Cuevas road through Hayner Resort, or by leaving the car at the entrance to Soledad Canyon farther south and hiking northeast over a low saddle. At the ruins of the old Dripping Springs Hotel, continue into the box canyon along a stream bed for several hundred yards until an exit is seen on a steep slope to the left. Climb out of the box canyon and follow the high canyon east and southeast (right) for a walk to the summit. The peak is named for a layer of grey-white rock which caps it. One normally returns the same way. The time from the Dripping Springs Hotel ruin is about 3 hours. Since Ice Canyon and parts of Soledad Canyon are on Fort Bliss land, and the Hayner Resort belongs to A. B. Cox, permission may have to be obtained to enter these areas.

Climbing Records

Most climbs in New Mexico can be accomplished at a leisurely pace which gives the climber sufficient time to enjoy the beautiful views, observe the vegetation, and study the rocks. Only a few of the longer climbs in the Sangre de Cristo Mountains require the ability of expert climbers to maintain a climbing speed of about 900' an hour. Several climbs have been made in 1964 which are remarkable because they were considerably faster than such speeds.

The speed record on the La Luz trail to Sandia Crest was broken in July, 1964, when Charles Floading from Sandia Base climbed to the top in 1 hr., 25 min., 20 sec. Only a month later Dean Rickerson from Los Alamos made the same climb in 1 hr., 8 min. Floading made the Wheeler Peak climb by way of Bull of the Woods Mountain in 2 hrs., 11 min., 20 sec., while Rickerson climbed by way of Williams Lake in 1 hr., 8 min. Dean Rickerson also holds the speed record for the climb of West Truchas from the boundary fence at the irrigation canal. His time in August, 1964, was 1 hr.

CAVES

The mountain area in New Mexico contains a great number of caves which have been explored wholly or in part, and others which still await exploration. From caves has come much of our evidence for early man in the western world and the association of ancient man with extinct animals.

There are relatively few caves north of Santa Fe. Starting with the Sandia Mountains, fault block ranges with thick limestone deposits extend south almost to the Texas border. These formations and related limestone reef structures such as occur in the Guadalupe Mountains have rocks with sufficiently high solubility in water so that ground water seeping into cracks can dissolve out cavities gradually and, over long periods of time, create caves and huge underground rooms. The action of melting snow and rain water filtering through the upper layers of already formed caves then leads to the formation of stalagtites, stalagmites, columns, and pillars. The finest examples of such caves are preserved in Carlsbad Caverns National Park.

Carlsbad Caverns. A cowboy named Jim White discovered the caverns in 1901 when he saw a cloud of bats coming out of a large dark pit from the side of a mountain in the Guadalupes. This proved to be the natural entrance to the caverns. The large deposits of bat guano which were found in the cave were mined for fertilizer. Jim White, who worked for the mining company, continued to explore the caverns and took visitors down. Through his efforts and the explorations of Dr. W. T. Lee of the U. S. Geological Survey, which were published in the **National Geographic,** the caverns were made a National Park in 1930.

Bones of extinct groundsloth and jaguar in the caverns indicate that there was an opening to the caves between 10,000 and 15,000 years ago. Nearby caves have yielded Basketmaker remains, and one sandal as well as pictographs have been found in the caverns. The enormous size of the caverns and the beauty of the formations makes Carlsbad Caverns unique in the state. The National Park Service schedules regularly conducted tours. In addition to the main caverns, there are other caves within the boundaries of the National Park which are accessible only by special permit. Among those located on Carlsbad Caverns West quad are: Ogle Cave and New Cave in Slaughter Canyon, Goat Cave in North Slaughter Canyon, and Whistling Cave and Painted Grotto in West Slaughter Canyon. Other caves which are said to be in the west fork of the canyon are: Guadalupe Cavern, Lake Cave, and Rainbow Cave. Carlsbad Caverns East quad shows Bat Cave and Chimney Cave.

Other caves around the headwaters of Dark Canyon are outside the boundaries of the National Park in the vicinity of Dark Lookout (6,950′), in Lincoln National Forest. Among these are: Cottonwood Cave, Hidden Cave, Black Cave, 2,000-Foot Cave, Rock Cave, and Hell-Below Cave.* There are also Indian paintings in this canyon. Cottonwood Cave (0.5 mile from the lookout), the most popular of the group, has stalagmites, soda straw stalagtites, pools of water, gypsum draperies, and cave pearls.

A hermit named James Pickett lived in a cave in Last Chance Canyon, named Hermit Cave. Investigations turned up many artifacts in the floor of this cave showing that others had lived there before him. The same canyon also contains a Goat Cave and a Cremation Cave with burial and ashes. Burnet Cave on the east side of the Guadalupes contained Basketmaker remains, bones of horse and camel, and Folsom points, together with bones of extinct bison and musk ox.

Fort Stanton Caves. Several caves in the vicinity of Fort

---

*Some caves are known by several names, others have the same name. As far as is known, those listed are different caves.

Stanton occur in San Andres limestone. Fort Stanton Cave is located halfway between Lincoln and Capitan, south of U.S. 380. The entrance is on a dirt road 3 miles east of Fort Stanton. The main cave has several miles of passages and crawlways which are dry today, but had so much water in them in the early 1900s that it was necessary to use a boat for exploring the cave. The entrance passage has bare walls partially blocked by cave-ins but about 2 miles from the mouth, rare types of selenite crystals are found. The most beautiful part is the "Hall of Velvet," so called because the walls look like velvet.

Fort Stanton Cave was apparently well-known to the Apache Indians. When U. S. cavalry chased some of them into the cave in 1862 and decided to starve them out, the same Indians were seen to steal their horses. They evidently escaped through a second entrance which has not been rediscovered to date.

Feather Cave (or Outlaw Cave) on the north side of the highway opposite the Fort Stanton Cave is almostly completely blackened by soot from many fires of the ancient inhabitants. A room discovered behind the main cave has yielded many artifacts, while several small shelter caves east of Feather Cave contained faded pictographs and pottery sherds. Smetnick Cave, also north of U. S. 380, has yielded many artifacts.

Sandia and Manzano Caves. The well-known Sandia Cave which has been discussed elsewhere is one of a group of limestone caves in Las Huertas Canyon in the Sandia Mountains. Manzano Cave, 5 miles west of Manzano, contained guano and some bola balls, while **Abo Cave** in the Manzano Mountains southwest of Abo and north of U.S. 60 (near Scholle) has pictographs.

Isleta Cave, 10 miles northwest of Isleta, the **Ice Caves** 27 miles southeast of Grants in the malpais, and the **Grenville Caves** 8 miles from Grenville are blowholes. Isleta Cave contained guano and bones dating to the Pleistocene period.

Gallina Cave in the San Pedro Parks Wild Area, 6 miles south of Gallina on State Road 96, is mainly a narrow passage along a small running stream. The upper of the two known

entrances is frequently blocked by beaver dams, the lower requires wading in cold water for 100′. Other entrances may have
been blocked by flash floods which followed ancient forest fires.
Burned pebbles, foreign to the region, and charcoal have been
found in the cave.

Alabaster Cave near San Ysidro is a tunnel-like winding cor-
ridor with alabaster walls, worn smooth by an ancient stream.

Jemez Cave, about 1 mile north of Jemez Springs, in the west
wall of Jemez Canyon (100′ above Soda Dam), contained the
mummified remains of a child, blankets, and sandals, dated about
1250 A.D.

Tres Hermanas (three sisters) **Cave,** one of the most spectacular caves in New Mexico, is located on the eastern slope of the
Tres Hermanas Mountains northwest of Columbus. It extends
300′ underground and is lined with uraniferous calcite and ara-
gonite, both fluorescing yellow-green and snow-white.

RIVER BOATING
(with contributions from J. H. Fretwell) *

The State of New Mexico is drained by five major rivers: the Rio Grande with its tributary the Pecos River; the San Juan and Gila Rivers, which belong to the Colorado System, and the Canadian River, which flows east into the Mississippi. Much of the water originates in the mountains of the state and some of the river gorges are in the vicinity of the mountains. For this reason it is considered appropriate to discuss the rivers and river boating in this Guide.

During the long past, before the turn of the century, the rivers of the region were regarded as obstacles and fording them during periods of high water was often a difficult feat. Ferryboats were used in some places, and eventually bridges were built. In more recent times, river boating has become a sport practiced during the spring runoff when the water is sufficiently high. Several persons have drowned while riding the rapids, however, and it is strongly advised that trips of this nature be undertaken only with proper equipment and experienced leaders.

The **Rio Grande** enters New Mexico at a region of former volcanic activity with extensive lava flows which once dammed up the waters and formed a lake which filled the San Luis Valley in Colorado. When the river cut through the basalt, it formed a canyon nearly 50 miles long and over 1,000' deep in places, which is called the "Taos Box," or "Rio Grande Box" (in part, on Taos and Vicinity quad). The upper Taos Box has many cataracts, low falls, and rapids, requiring portaging in the four miles upstream from the Red River confluence. Frank T. Garcia of Albuquerque drowned here May 9, 1970, while attempting a rubber raft descent.

---

* Mr. J. H. "Stretch" Fretwell, at 4091 Trinity Drive, Los Alamos, New Mexico 87544, would be happy to assist with questions about proposed river boating trips.

It has a vertical drop of 55′ per mile and is for experts only. The run starts at Lobatos Bridge, 13 miles east of Antonito, Colorado, and goes 43 miles downstream to Dunn's Bridge, 2 miles west of Arroyo Hondo. At the confluence of the Red River it passes the Rio Grande Gorge Recreation Area.

The next 15 miles to Taos Junction Bridge on State Road 96, in the lower Taos Box, are difficult but not so steep as the upper section. A short distance from Dunn's Bridge the river flows past American Hot Springs, the site of an old bridge and abandoned spa. A little farther down river a new highway bridge from Taos has been built across the gorge. While the start of the trip is easy, the river gradually drops more steeply and flows through a number of rapids and cataracts until it reaches the Taos Junction Bridge. From there it levels out again for the 6 miles to Pilar.

In the 5-mile stretch below Pilar, U.S. 64 has crowded the river into a narrow channel with long rapids and sharp rocks. A white water race against time is held here during high water in May. From the Taos County line to Velarde, the Rio Grande has no major rapids. The valley widens at Velarde and the river flows slowly to the Otowi Bridge with several low irrigation dams crossing the river diagonally. These are the only major obstacles and they are best crossed at the upstream end.

The White Rock Canyon trip starting at Otowi Bridge on State Road 4 is one of the most popular in the state. The trip can be made in one day, although some people have camped near Frijoles Canyon, using two days. While the average drop of the White Rock Canyon run is about 10′ per mile, the drop is nearly 40′ per mile at Ancho Canyon Rapids. This spectacular run on the Rio has 1,200′ high basalt walls topped with white pumice and tuff, for which the canyon is named. There are rapids at each of the major side canyons: in descending order these are at Buckmann, Pajarito Canyon, Water Canyon, Capulin Canyon, and Sanchez Canyon. A boatman's register has been placed on a large cottonwood tree on the west bank of Ancho Canyon rapid. At this difficult rapid which is a long "S" turn, Don Bender of Albuquerque drowned in 1961. Three companions managed to swim ashore after their raft capsized.

Below Cochiti, numerous diversion dams take increasing amounts of water from the Rio Grande so that now the river bed is completely dry during the summer months, from 10 miles above Albuquerque. In years past there was considerably more water in the lower valley. In the 1880's, in a year of high water, an early editor freighted his furniture and also his wife down the river from Albuquerque to Socorro. He made the trip in 2½ days and for 9 miles was able to keep up with a railroad train rolling along the bank. In the same year a liquor dealer floated two boatloads of beer downstream to a railroad crew.

Harvey Fergusson made the river trip from Albuquerque to Socorro twice. In 1922 he took a flatboat there in three days, partly rowing and partly pushing. In 1929 he traveled the river from Otowi Bridge to Bernalillo in a folding canvas boat.

Extensive straightening and channelization has been done on the Rio Grande in the vicinity of Socorro by the U.S. Corps of Engineers, so the river is not interesting to boaters. Below Cabillo dam there is a "rebirth" of the Rio Grande during the summer irrigation season with good flows toward Las Cruces.

The **Pecos River** can be run during periods of high water from Pecos as far as Anton Chico and Santa Rosa. From Cowles to Terrero the river is clear, cold, and quite steep, and many rocks and logs make the upper part a difficult white water trip. From Terrero the grade becomes less steep and irrigation dams begin to appear. Eventually the Pecos meanders and flows at a gentle pace, where the canyon widens to a valley below Anton Chico.

The **Chama River,** a small tributary of the Rio Grande, provides one of the best wilderness runs from the fishing camp below El Vado Dam to the private bridge near Gallina Bench Ranch, almost 18 miles downstream. Above the mouth of the Gallina River, good camping spots are accessible only by boat. From Abiquiu to Espanola the river moves rapidly, crossing numerous irrigation dams. Occasional barbed wire fences run across the river. Rapids 4 miles downstream from Medanales and the irrigation dam 1 mile above the Chamita Bridge should be treated with caution. The stream flow in the Chama River should improve considerably when San Juan River water is diverted on a continuing basis.

The **San Juan River** is controlled by Navajo Dam within the State of New Mexico. The run below the dam to Blanco is the best. Continuing downstream the river meanders with numerous large compound islands and some irrigation dams. Downstream from Shiprock, the San Juan develops curious "sandwaves" 3-4' high, during spring floods.

The **Gila River** had clear water as late as 1870. During the years of 1885-1900 when there were close to one million cattle in the territory, the range was overgrazed. Years of drought and occassional floods which followed have transformed the Gila into a muddy river as it leaves New Mexico's western border.

Starting in the Gila Wilderness area the river is still clear. During the spring run off or after heavy rains there is adequate water. Overnight float trips start where State Road 527 crosses the Gila south of Gila Cliff Dwellings National Monument. The river is steep and tricky until Sapillo Creek is crossed and the valley widens. Most trips terminate at the confluence with Mongollon Creek 10 miles northwest of Cliff, before irrigation dams deplete the river.

The **Canadian River** is infrequently run during unusually high spring runoff from Taylor Springs on U.S. 56 through sandstone canyons to Sabinoso, although some trips continue to Conchas Reservoir.

Unfortunately, much of the spring crest from the Cimarron River, a major tributary to the Canadian River, is removed by the dam at Eagle Nest.

Recommended books for river runners which form an excellent basic library are: the American National Red Cross's *Canoeing* (Garden City, N.Y.); Robert E. McNair's *Basic River Canoeing* (American Camping Association, Bradford Woods, Martinsville, Ind.); and John T. Urban's *A White Water Handbook for Canoe and Kayak* (Appalachian Mountain Club, Boston, Mass.).

WINTER MOUNTAINEERING

The mountains in southern New Mexico, with exception of Sierra Blanca, normally receive little snow and winter climbing is feasible without appreciable difficulties. It should be remembered that snow is likely to be encountered on the north slopes and that shaded gullies may have ice in them. The higher northern mountains usually have appreciable snowfall during the winter months. The temperature can drop to below zero in the high altitudes. Strong winds should be expected on the higher ridges, and the general climate is not much different from that in the mountains of Colorado or other states farther north. Mountaineering under such conditions requires special equipment as well as experience, and caution is advisable.

The first recorded winter climb in the New Mexico mountains was made in March, 1928, by Forest Ranger J. W. Johnson and Forest Service Inspector of Grazing, D. A. Shoemaker, who climbed South Truchas from Beatty's Cabin on 8' skis in 14.5 hours. Snowshoeing in the high country was probably done even earlier, but the first published record of snowshoeing was in 1933 in the Sandia Mountains. Graeme McGowan used 6'9" cross-country skis in 1935 to climb Lake Peak from Aspen Ranch, and Perl Charles skied, in 1939-40, over most of the high country of the upper Pecoes including the Santa Barbara divide, Truchas Peak, and Pecos Baldy.

The high country is most accessible in the vicinity of the winter sports areas because a special effort is made by the state to keep the roads open. There are at present 5 major ski areas in New Mexico: Santa Fe Basin in Santa Fe National Forest; Red

River and Taos in Carson National Forest; Sierra Blanca in Lincoln National Forest; and Sandia Peak in Cibola National Forest. Smaller ones are located near Tres Ritos (Sipapu) in Carson National Forest, on Pajarito Mountain near Los Alamos, and near Cloudcroft in Lincoln National Forest. All of these are located at 8,000'-12,000' because reliable snow is found only at these altitudes. The major areas have lodges with good accomodations, and some have become famous for fine food. Cross-country skiing, snowshoeing, and winter mountaineering can be undertaken by experienced groups by starting from one of these areas. They will be strictly on their own and need to be fully equipped.

In the northern Sangre de Cristo Mountains, winter trips have been made to Gold Hill and Williams Lake by the standard routes from Twining. Several parties have made the traverse from Twining to Red River via Gold Hill along the Goose Lake road. Farther south, Lake Peak, Santa Fe Baldy, and Truchas Peak have been climbed in mid-winter. Lake Peak is a pleasant easy trip through the woods east of the ski area, with one fairly steep section at the head of the old cirque. Santa Fe Baldy by way of the Winsor trail is considerably longer, requiring a full day in favorable weather. Truchas Peak normally requires 2-3 days. There are two recorded winter climbs of South Truchas Peak from Cowles by way of the Pecos Baldy-Truchas ridge. Other attempts from the west side through the Quemado Valley have led as far the Truchas Amphitheater but not to any of the summits. It is believed, however, that any serious attempt from this side would be successful.

Snowshoe trips along the Winsor trail from the Santa Fe Ski Basin to Cowles have been reported and others from the Rio Medio Valley to the Lone Tree (Truchas) Lakes. From the Los Alamos Ski Area, regular winter trips have been made to the rim of the Valle Grande, to the summits of Pajarito Mountain, and along the Pipeline Road. Pajarito Mountain is a relatively easy trip from the saddle overlooking Valle Grande. Return trips via the other summit or Valle Canyon are alternatives for the descent route. A somewhat longer trip uses the jeep road over Rincon

Bonito (Rincon Bonito trail) to the north of the ski area and return by way of the Pipeline Road which enters Los Alamos at North Road. Trips of this sort can be done safely if the groups undertaking them are properly equipped.

It should be borne in mind that it is difficult to cover even 10 miles in one day in deep soft snow, particularly if much change in altitude is involved. Most of the touring is done in early spring when the snow is consolidated and climbing is less difficult. If any rock climbing is contemplated, equipment such as rope and ice axe is essential. There are no local guides in the region, as they are found in the Alps, but the climbing clubs usually have experienced men and schedule some trips in the winter months. There have been two fatalities on a winter trip to the Truchas Mountains which might have been avoided if proper equipment had been available and a different route had been chosen.

Skiing

This popular sport came to New Mexico only recently. The first ski practice hills were established at Hyde Park (8,500'), in Evergreen Valley (8,400'), and west of the Los Alamos Boys School (9,300') in 1936. Hyde Park, northeast of Santa Fe, became the first real winter sports area in the state in the following year. The Hyde Memorial Park, which once was a homestead, was bought by the Boy Scout Leader, B. T. B. Hyde, and was given to the State of New Mexico by his family in 1936. The ski area was moved to the Big Tesuque drainage in 1946.

A similar development took place shortly afterwards on the east slope of the Sandia Mountains. The Albuquerque Ski Club was organized by Bob Nordhaus in 1937. Its first winter sports area at Tree Spring was so successful that it was moved to a better location at La Madera, where T-bar lifts were installed in 1946. Not to be outdone, the Santa Fe Winter Sports Club pushed for a tow in the Aspen Basin, discovered by G. McGowan. The Tesuque Indians opposed the construction of a road into this basin, which was their sacred area, but stood little chance against the

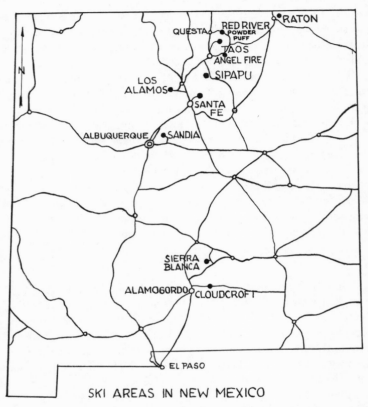

SKI AREAS IN NEW MEXICO

ski enthusiasts. A double-chair lift was built in 1950, supposedly from the towers and buckets of an old mine.

The Taos Ski Valley was discovered in the 1950s by Ernie Blake, manager of ski lifts in Santa Fe and Colorado, on his flights between the two areas.

The Sierra Blanca Recreation Area has changed hands recently and is now owned and operated by the Mescalero Apache Indian Tribe.

A brief description of the areas and their facilities is given in the following.

Raton Ski Basin (7,500') 12 miles northeast of Raton on paved State Road 72 (one mile of gravel road), has at present a 1,300' Poma lift, beginners' and intermediate slopes, and a day lodge overlooking the lower slopes.

Red River Ski Area (8,750') in Carson National Forest is located at the resort town of Red River, 13 miles east of Questa on paved State Road 38. A 6200' double-chair lift rises to an elevation of 10,274'. In addition there are a 950' double-chair lift, an Alpine Platter lift, an 800' Poma lift, and a 300' Baby Poma lift for beginners. There are 14 miles of skiing trails and a restaurant atop the mountain. Motel accommodations and restaurants can be found in the town of Red River.

Powder Puff Mountain Ski Area (8,750') caters to the beginner, but also has runs for the intermediate skier. Located ½ mile west of Red River on paved State Road 38, it has a double-chair lift, a Poma lift, and 2 rope tows, 350' vertical ascent. Snack bar and snow-making equipment are provided. Lodging facilities are available at Red River.

Singing River Ski Area (8,000') 4½ miles northeast of Questa on all-weather State Road 563 has a 600' ski run with 2 rope tows, and 2 slopes for other winter sports. Slopes are lighted for evening enjoyment. Reservations are required for day skiers or for overnight accommodations in cabin units or lodge with family-style meals.

Taos Ski Valley (9,412') at the old mining town of Twining, 19 miles from the Taos Plaza on State Road 150 (9 miles of improved gravel road) has 4 double-chair lifts which rise 2,900 vertical feet and 4 Poma lifts. There are more than 20 miles of challenging ski trails with 33 slopes up to 6 miles long. Accommodations include restaurants, sauna and heated swimming pool, lodges, and condominiums at Twining.

Angel Fire Ski Area (8,400'), 25 miles east of Taos on paved all-weather U.S. 64 (12 miles south of Eagle Nest) has 3 double-chair lifts rising to an elevation of 10,680'. Two beginners areas are served by separate chair lifts. Accommodations include a lodge and condominium apartments.

Sipapau Ski Area (8,182′) and Lodge are located on State Highway 3, 3 miles west of Tres Ritos, or 25 miles from Taos, on paved road. Facilities include 2 Poma lifts with a maximum vertical rise of 437′. Accommodations consist of cabins, dormitories, trailer space, and a restaurant and cafeteria adjacent to the tows.

Los Alamos Ski Area (9,200′) on the north side of Pajarito Mountain is 5 miles west of Los Alamos. It has 9 miles of trails served by a 3,800′ long T-bar lift with a vertical rise of 1,100′ and a double-chair lift with an uphill capacity of 1,200 skiers per hour. A pair of rope tows handles the two beginners' areas. Accommodations include a warming house, a sun deck, and a snack bar.

Santa Fe Ski Basin (10,300′) is 16 miles from Santa Fe on a paved road. There are 4 lifts—2 double-chair, one 4,200′ long, and 2 Poma lifts. The greatest vertical rise is approximately 2,000′ and the higest terminal is 12,047′. There are 700 acres of skiing terrain and trails. Accommodations in the basin consist of a lodge and restaurant, and cafeteria. Bus service from Santa Fe is provided.

Sandia Peak Ski Area (8,628′) 29 miles from Albuquerque by way of Interstate 40, State Roads 10 and 44, has 2 double-chair lifts, a T-bar, and 3 other lifts serving 15 miles of trails and open slopes, with up to 1,750′ vertical rise. There are restaurants at the top (10,378′) and bottom of the slopes. A ten-minute spectacular 2.7-mile aerial tramway operates from the valley on the west side of the Sandia Mountains 5.5 miles east of Tramway Road Exit from Interstate 25.

Sierra Blanca Ski Resort (9,700′), 16 miles northwest of Ruidoso on paved highway at the base of Sierra Blanca Peak, has 3 T-bar lifts, 2 Poma lifts, and a gondola tramway to the summit of Lookout Peak (1,700′ vertical rise to 11,400′). The resort has open slopes and ski trails and restaurants at upper and lower terminals. Numerous accommodations are found in Ruidoso.

Cloudcroft Ski Area (9,000′) 19 miles east of Alamogordo on State Road 82 features a T-Bar, a Poma lift, and a Mitey Mite portable lift up to 1,000′ long. There are 11 slopes, with night skiing provided. Accommodations and restaurants are available in Cloudcroft, 3 miles way.

REFERENCES TO THE LITERATURE

Geology

Dutton, C. E., Sixth Annual Report of the U.S. Geological Survey 1884-1885.

Harley, G. T., The Geology and Ore Deposits of Sierra County, New Mexico, Bulletin 10 of the State Bureau of Mines and Mineral Resources, Socorro, 1934.

Hayden, F. V., First, Second, and Third Geological and Geographical Reports of the Territories for 1867-1869, Washington, D. C., 1873.

Kottlowski, F. E., Flower, R. H., Thompson, M. L., and Foster, R. W., Stratigraphic Studies of the San Andres Mountains, Bureau of Mines and Mineral Resources, Socorro, N. M., 1956.

McKinlay, R. F., Geology of Costilla and Latir Peak Quadrangle, Taos County, N. M., Bulletin 42 of the State Bureau of Mines and Mineral Resources, Socorro, N. M., 1956.

Macomb, Capt. J. N., Report of the Exploring Expedition from Santa Fé, New Mexico, to the Junction of the Grand and Green Rivers of the Great Colorado of the West, in 1859, Government Printing Office, Washington, 1876. (First account of Shiprock, called the Needles, with a good account and drawing of the ascent of Pedernal near Abiquiu.)

Miller, J. P., Montgomery, A., and Sutherland, P. K., Geology of Part of the Southern Sangre de Cristo Mountains, State Bureau of Mines and Mineral Resources, Socorro, N. M., 1964.

New Mexico Geological Society, Guidebooks.

San Juan Basin, north and east sides	1950
San Juan Basin, south and west sides	1951
Rio Grande Country, Central New Mexico	1952
Southwestern New Mexico	1953
Southeastern New Mexico	1954
South-central New Mexico	1955

Southeastern Sangre de Cristo Mountains   1956
West-central New Mexico   1959
Rio Chama Country   1960
Albuquerque Country   1961
Socorro Region   1963
Ruidoso Country   1964

New Mexico Geological Society, Scenic Trips to the Geologic Past.

Baldwin, B., and Kottlowski, F. E., Santa Fe, N. M., 1955.

Schilling, J. H., Taos-Red River-Eagle Nest, 1956.

Allen, J. E., and Kottlowski, F. E., Roswell-Capitan-Ruidoso, and Bottomless Lakes Park, 1958.

Foster, R. W., Southern Zuni Mountains, 1958.

Schilling, J. H., Silver City-Santa Rita-Hurley, 1959.

Montgomery, A., and Sutherland, P. K., Trail Guide to the Upper Pecos, 1960.

Muehlberger, W. R., and Foster, R. W., High Plains-Northeastern New Mexico, 1961.

Christiansen, P. W., and Kottlowski, F. E., Mosaic of New Mexico's Scenery, Rocks, and History, 1964.

Kelley, Vincent C., Albuquerque: Its Mountains, Valley, Water, and Volcanoes, Bureau of Mines and Mineral Resources, Socorro, N.M., 1969.

Wheeler, G. M., Annual Report on the Geographical Exploration and Surveys West of the 100th Meridian, Washington, D. C., 1875-1881.

Anthropology and Archaeology

Agogino, G. A., Rouner, I., and Irwin-Williams, C., Early Man in the New World, Science *143,* 1352, 1964.

Harrington, J. P., The Ethnogeography of the Tewa Indians, Bureau of American Ethnology, Government Printing Office, Washington, 1916.

Hewett, E. L., Ancient Life in the American Southwest, Tudor Publishing Company, New York, 1948.

Hewett, E. L., The Pajarito Plateau and its Ancient People, University of New Mexico Press, 1953.

Hibben, F. C., The Lost Americans, Crowell, New York, 1946.

Kidder, A. V., An Introduction to the Study of Southwestern Archaeology, Yale University Press, New Haven, Conn., 1924.

Kidder, A. V., The Pottery of Pecos, Yale University Press, New Haven, Conn., 1931 and 1936.

McGregor, J. C., Southwestern Archaeology, John Wiley and Sons, New York, 1941.

Smiley, T. L., Stubbs, S. A., and Bannister, B., A Foundation for the Dating of Some Late Archaeological Sites in the Rio Grande Area, Univ. of Arizona Bulletin XXIV, No. 3, 1953.

Stallings, N. S., Jr., A Tree Ring Chronology for the Rio Grande Drainage, National Academy of Science, Proceedings 19, No. 9, 1953.

Wormington, H. M., Prehistoric Indians of the Southwest, 3rd Edition, The Denver Museum of Natural History, 1956.

Recorded History

Bancroft, H. H., History of Arizona and New Mexico, Horn and Wallace, Albuquerque, N. M., 1962.

Bolton, H. E., Coronado, Knight of Pueblo and Plain, Whittlesey House, New York, 1949.

Bolton, H. E., Coronado and the Turquoise Trail, University of New Mexico Press, Albuquerque, 1949.

Bolton, H. E., Spanish Exploration in the Southwest, 1542-1706, Barnes and Noble, New York, 1952.

Calvin, R., River of the Sun, University of New Mexico Press, Albuquerque, 1946.

Charles, Mrs. T., Tales of Tularosa, Alamogordo, N. M., 1954.

Coan, C. F., A Shorter History of New Mexico, Edwards Brothers, Ann Arbor, Michigan, 1928.

Connelly, W. E., Bryant and Douglas, Doniphan's Expedition, Book and Stationery Company, Kansas City, Missouri, 1907.

Espinosa, J. M., First Expedition of Vargas into New Mexico, University of New Mexico Press, Albuquerque, 1940.

Espinosa, J. M., Crusaders of the Rio Grande, Inst. Jesuit History, 1942.

Ferguson, E., New Mexico, A Pageant of Three Peoples, Alfred Knopf, New York, 1951.

Gilpin, L., The Rio Grande, River of Destiny, Duell, Sloan and Pierce, New York, 1949.

Gregg, J., The Commerce of the Prairies, Edited by M. L. Moorhead, University of Oklahoma Press, 1954.

Hackett, C. W., The Pueblo Revolt, University of New Mexico Press, Albuquerque, 1942.

Hammond, G. P., Don Juan Oñate and the Founding of New Mexico, Historical Society of New Mexico, Albuquerque, 1927.

Hammond, G. P., and Rey, A., Narratives of the Coronado Expedition, University of New Mexico Press, Albuquerque, 1940.

Hammond, G. P., and Rey, A., Oñate, First Colonizer of New Mexico, University of New Mexico Press, Albuquerque, 1953.

Hodge, F. W., and Rey, A., The Benavides Memorial, University of New Mexico Press, Albuquerque, 1945.

Horgan, P., The Great River, Rinehart and Company, New York, 1954.

Horgan, P., The Centuries of Sante Fe, E. P. Dutton and Company, New York, 1956.

James, H., The Curse of the San Andres, Pageant Press, New York, 1953.

McNitt, Frank, editor, Navaho Expedition, University of Oklahoma Press, Norman, 1964.

Morang, A., Santa Fe, Sage Books, Denver, Colorado, 1947.

Prince, L. B., Concise History of New Mexico, Torch Press, 1914.

Quaife, M. M., The Southwestern Expedition of Zebulon M. Pike, The Lakeside Press, Chicago, 1925.

Reeve, F. D., New Mexico, A Short, Illustrated History, Sage Books, Denver, 1964.

Reno, P., Taos Pueblo, Sage Books, Denver, 1963.

Sonnichsen, C. L., Tularosa, Devin-Adair, New York, 1960.

Thomas, A. B., The Plains Indians and New Mexico, University of New Mexico Press, Albuquerque, 1940.

Twitchell, R. E., Leading Facts of New Mexican History, Torch Press, Cedar Rapids, Iowa, 1912.

Vestal, S., The Old Santa Fe Trail, Houghton Mifflin Company, Boston, 1939.

Watson, D., The Pinos Altos Story, Enterprise, Silver City, N. M., 1960.

Climate and Vegetation

Arnberger, L. P., and Janish, J. R., Flowers of the Southwest Mountains, Fourth Edition, Southwestern Monuments Association, Globe, Arizona, 1968.

Calvin, R., Sky Determines, University of New Mexico Press, Albuquerque, 1948.

Craighead, J. J. and F. C., Jr., and Davis, R. J., A Field Guide to Rocky Mountain Wildflowers, Houghton Mifflin, 1963.

Dodge, N. N., and Janish, J. R., Flowers of the Southwest Deserts, Southwestern Monuments Association, Six Edition, Globe, Arizona, 1965.

Little, E. L., Jr., Southwestern Trees, Department of Agriculture, Superintendent of Documents, Washington, D. C., 1950.

Patraw, P. M., and Janish, J. R., Flowers of the Southwest Mesas, Southwestern Monuments Association, Fourth Edition, Globe, Arizona, 1964.

Peterson, R. T., A Field Guide to Western Birds, Revised Edition, Houghton Mifflin, Boston, 1961.

Preston, R. J., Jr., Rocky Mountain Trees, Second Revised Edition, Dover Publications, New York, 1968.

Wildlife

Bailey, F. M., Birds of New Mexico, New Mexico Department
    of Game and Fish, Sante Fe, N. M., 1928.

Bailey, V., Mammals of New Mexico, U. S. Department of Agri-
    culture, Superintendent of Documents, Washington 25, D. C.,
    1931.

Barker, E., Beatty's Cabin, The University of New Mexico Press,
    Albuquerque, 1953.

Edwords, C. E., Campfires of a Naturalist, D. Appleton Com-
    pany, 1893.

Emory, W. H., Notes of a Military Reconnaissance from Fort
    Leavenworth in Missouri to San Diego, California, 1848.

Ligon, J. S., Wildlife of New Mexico (Game Survey of 1926 and
    1927), New Mexico Department of Game and Fish, Santa
    Fe, N. M., 1927.

Ligon, J. S., New Mexico Birds, University of New Mexico
    Press, Albuquerque, 1961.

Olin, G., and Bierly, E., Mammals of the Southwest Mountains
    and Mesas, Southwestern Monuments Association, Globe,
    Arizona, 1961.

Mineral Resources

Lasky, S. G., and Wootton, T. P., The Metallic Resources of New
    Mexico, Bulletin No. 7, New Mexico School of Mines, So-
    corro, 1933.

Northrup, S. A., Minerals of New Mexico, Revised Edition, Uni-
    versity of New Mexico Press, Albuquerque, 1959.

Robbins, Royal, Basic Rockcraft, La Siesta Press, Glendale,
    California, 1971.

Simpson, B. W., New Mexico Gem Trails, Gem Trail Publishing
    Company, Granbury, Texas, 1961.

Talmage, S. B., and Wootton, T. P., The Non-metallic Mineral
    Resources of New Mexico, Bulletin No. 12, New Mexico
    School of Mines, Socorro, 1937.

Exploring the High Country

Abert, J. W., Abert's New Mexico Report, 1846-1847, Horn and Wallace, Albuquerque, N. M., 1962.

Barker, E., Beatty's Cabin, The University of New Mexico Press, Albuquerque, 1953.

Barker, E., When the Dogs Bark 'Treed,' University of New Mexico Press, Albuquerque, 1946.

Barker, O., and Barker, E., The Hermit of the Mountain, New Mexico Quarterly, XXXI, No. 4, 349, 1961-1962.

Douglass, W. B., Proceedings of the 1915 Meeting of the International Congress of Americanists, page 344, Washington, D. C., 1917.

Gregory, H. E., Geology of the Navajo Country, U. S. Geological Survey Prof. Paper 93, Washington, D. C., 1917.

Hayden, F. V., Notes on the Geology of New Mexico, 1876.

Hewett, E. L., and Dutton, B. P., The Pueblo Indian World, University of New Mexico Press, Albuquerque, 1945.

Hewett, E. L., and Mauzy, W. L., Landmarks of New Mexico, University of New Mexico Press, Albuquerque, 1947.

Kline, L. G., editor, Guide to the Sandia Mountains, privately published, Albuquerque, 1970.

Lavender, D., The Big Divide, Doubleday and Company, Inc., Garden City, New York, 1948.

Mader, C., Climbing in the Pecos High Country, Summit Magazine IV, No. 5, 2, 1958.

Maise, A. Q., Dawn Patrol of Young Scientists, Readers Digest, November Issue, 145, 1956.

Marcou, J., Report on the Geology of the Route, Whipple's Reconnaissance near the 35th Parallel, U. S. 33rd Congress, 2nd Sess., Senate Exec. Doc. 78 and House Exec. Doc. 91, v. 3, pt. 4, p. 121-164, 1856.

McKenna, J. A., Black Range Tales, Wilson-Erickson, Inc., New York, 1936.

Reno, P., And Farther on Was Gold in Twining, Sage Books, Denver, Colorado, 1962.

Stamm, R. A., High Country Pedestrian, New Mexico Magazine, *26*, p. 18, July, 1948.

Ungnade, H. E., Archaeological Finds in the Sangre de Cristo Mountains of New Mexico, El Palacio, *70*, No. 4, p. 15, 1963.

Walter, H. D., My Friends, the Mountains, New Mexico Magazine, *27*, p. 24, August, 1949.

Wendorf, F., and Miller, J. P., Artifacts from High Mountain Sites in the Sangre de Cristo Range, New Mexico, El Palacio, *66*, No. 2, p. 37, 1958.

General References

American Guide Series, New Mexico, A Guide to the Colorful State, Hasting House, New York, 1940.

Forrest, E. R., With a Camera in Old Navaholand, University of Oklahoma Press, Norman, 1970.

Mann, E. B., and Harvey, F. E., New Mexico, Land of Enchantment, Michigan State University Press, East Lansing, 1955.

Numerous descriptive articles and isolated facts concerning the mountain areas of New Mexico are found in New Mexico Magazine and in El Palacio, the Journal of the Museum of New Mexico. Other stories and items of current interest are frequently given in the local newspapers, including The Albuquerque Journal, The Albuquerque Tribune, Las Vegas Daily Optic, The Los Alamos Monitor, and The New Mexican.

Pearce, T. M., New Mexico Place Names, University of New Mexico Press, Albuquerque, 1965.

INDEX OF NAMED SUMMITS

Mountain	Altitude (feet)	Range (or Region)
Wheeler Peak	13,160	Taos
Old Mike	13,135	Taos
South Truchas	13,102	Santa Fe
Middle Truchas	13,070	Santa Fe
West Truchas	13,066	Santa Fe
North Truchas	13,024	Santa Fe
Big Costilla Peak	13,005	Taos
Jicarilla	12,944	Santa Fe
Simpson Peak	12,850	Taos
Jicarita	12,750	Mora
Latir Peak	12,723	Taos
Gold Hill	12,682	Taos
Santa Barbara	12,641	Mora
Santa Fe Baldy	12,622	Santa Fe
Sheepshead	12,600	Santa Fe
Vallecito Mountain	12,600	Taos
Virsylvia Peak	12,600	Taos
Little Costilla Peak	12,580	Cimarron
East Pecos Baldy	12,529	Santa Fe
West Pecos Baldy	12,500	Santa Fe
Cabresto Peak	12,462	Taos
Venado Peak	12,447	Taos
Baldy Mountain	12,441	Cimarron
Lew Wallace Peak	12,438	Taos
Lake Peak	12,409	Santa Fe
Pueblo Peak	12,282	Taos

215

Taos Cone	12,277	Taos
Penitente Peak	12,249	Santa Fe
Capulin Peak	12,200	Santa Fe
Trampas Mountain	12,175	Santa Fe
Frazer Mountain	12,150	Taos
Lobo Peak	12,106	Taos
Tesuque Peak	12,047	Santa Fe
Touch-me-not Mountain	12,045	Cimarron
Baldy Mountain	12,043	Taos
Sierra Blanca Peak	12,003	Sierra Blanca
Larkspur Peak	12,000	Taos
Pinabete Peak	11,953	Taos
Cerro Vista	11,947	Mora
Flag Mountain	11,938	Taos
Cerro Olla	11,925	Mora
Sierra Mosca	11,801	Santa Fe
Relica Peak	11,784	Taos
Bunkhouse Bare Point	11,730	Cimarron
Clear Creek Mountain	11,711	Cimarron
Tunnel Hill	11,670	Taos
Elk Mountain	11,661	Las Vegas
Bull of the Woods Mtn.	11,610	Taos
Tschicoma Mountain	11,561	Jemez
Spring Mountain	11,500	Las Vegas
Lookout Peak	11,400	Sierra Blanca
Cuchillo de Fernando	11,390	Taos
Comanche Peak	11,326	Cimarron
Mount Taylor	11,301	San Mateo
Brazos Peak	11,288	Brazos
Black Mountain	11,286	Taos
La Cueva Peak	11,265	Mora
Redondo Peak	11,254	Jemez
Polvadera Peak	11,232	Jemez
Van Diest Peak	11,222	Taos
Taos Peak	11,220	Taos
Ortiz Peak	11,185	Taos

Aspen Peak	11,109	Santa Fe
Agua Fria Peak	11,086	Cimarron
Angel Fire Mountain	11,060	Cimarron
La Mosca	11,036	San Mateo
Peñasco Mountain	10,970	Mora
Sawmill Mountain	10,936	Taos
San Antonio Peak	10,935	(N.-cen. N. M.)
Garcia Peak	10,925	Cimarron
Gallina Peak	10,893	Taos
Black Mountain	10,892	Cimarron
Whitewater Baldy	10,892	Mogollon
Osha Mountain	10,885	Rincon
Picuris Mountain	10,810	Picuris
Tetilla Peak	10,800	Taos
Mogollon Peak	10,778	Mogollon
Jawbone Mountain	10,680	(N.-cen. N. M.)
Sandia Crest	10,678	Sandia
Bear Mountain	10,663	Cimarron
South Baldy	10,640	Magdalena
Bonito Peak	10,616	Cimarron
Cieneguilla Mountain	10,613	Cimarron
Santa Fe Dome	10,613	Santa Fe
Round Mountain	10,600	Santa Fe
San Pedro Peaks	10,577	Nacimiento
Thompson Peak	10,554	Santa Fe
Center Baldy	10,532	Mogollon
Rosilla Peak	10,500	Las Vegas
Caballo Mountain	10,496	Jemez
Cimarroncito Peak	10,468	Cimarron
Casita Piedra Peak	10,453	Taos
Cerro Rubio	10,449	Jemez
Sandia Peak	10,447	Sandia
Pajarito Mountain	10,441	Jemez
Knob	10,400	Mora
Brokeoff Mountain	10,365	(N.-cen. N. M.)
Sierra del Don Fernando	10,363	Fernando

Blue Mountain	10,325	San Mateo
Vick's Peak	10,290	San Mateo
Trail Peak	10,242	Cimarron
Cerrito Colorado	10,235	Fernando
Cerro Grande	10,199	Jemez
Glorieta Baldy	10,199	Santa Fe
Apache Peak	10,164	Taos
Ute Peak	10,151	(N.-cen. N. M.)
Tusas Mountain	10,150	(N.-cen. N. M.)
San Mateo Peak	10,141	San Mateo
Grouse Mountain	10,132	Mogollon
Mount Withington	10,116	San Mateo
Cerro Pelado	10,112	Jemez
Thumb	10,107	Sandia
Capulin Peak	10,104	Taos
Manzano Peak	10,098	Manzano
Capitan Peak	10,083	Capitan
Hermit Peak	10,060	Las Vegas
Reeds Peak	10,012	Black
Diamond Peak	10,011	Black
Hillsboro Peak	10,011	Black
Osha Peak	10,003	Manzano
El Cielo	10,000	Las Vegas
Grass Mountain	10,000	Santa Fe
Mon Jeau	10,000	Sierra Blanca
Willow Mountain	9,993	Mogollon
Nogal Peak	9,950	Sierra Blanca
Burn Peak	9,938	Cimarron
Rabbit Mountain	9,938	Jemez
Los Griegos	9,933	Jemez
Lookout Peak	9,922	Cimarron
Bearwallow Mountain	9,920	Mogollon
Cerro Pedernal	9,862	Jemez
North Baldy	9,858	Magdalena
West Baldy	9,806	Mogollon
Rayado Peak	9,805	Cimarron

Eagle Peak	9,802	Tularosa
South Sandia Peak	9,782	Sandia
Elk Mountain	9,780	Elk
Nacimiento Peak	9,761	Nacimiento
Crater Peak	9,748	Cimarron
Grassy	9,679	San Mateo
Sawyers Peak	9,668	Black
Carrizo Mountain	9,656	Sacramento
Mangas Mountain	9,650	Mangas
Cross-O Mountain	9,619	Black
Mining Mountain	9,617	Jemez
Bosque Peak	9,610	Manzano
Madre Mountain	9,585	Datil
Mosca Peak	9,509	Manzano
Guadalupe Peak	9,450	Manzano
Luera Peak	9,420	Luera
O Bar O Mountain	9,410	(Gila Natl. Forest)
Shaefers Peak	9,400	Cimarron
Capilla Peak	9,375	Manzano
Cerro Pelon	9,367	Jemez
Davenport Peak	9,355	Datil
Sunset Peak	9,320	Capitan
Black Mountain	9,303	(Gila Natl. Forest)
Barillas Peak	9,300	Las Vegas
Mount Sedgwick	9,256	Zuni
Sacramento Peak	9,250	Sacramento
Ruiz Peak	9,208	Jemez
Pelona Mountain	9,204	(Gila Riv. Drng.)
Ladron Peak	9,176	Ladron
Atalaya Mountain	9,121	Santa Fe
Jim Smith Peak	9,100	(Spur Lake Basin)
North Peak	9,069	Magdalena
Elk Mountain	9,058	Elk
Pajarito Peak	9,042	Nacimiento
Black Peak	9,025	Pinos Altos
Organ Needle	9,012	Organ

Grizzly Tooth	9,005	Cimarron
Tooth of Time	9,003	Cimarron
Signal Peak	9,001	Pinos Altos
Crosby Mountain	9,000	Datil
Gallina Peak	8,977	(N.-cen. N. M.)
Salinas Peak	8,958	San Andres
Fox Mountain	8,950	Gallo
Lilly Mountain	8,934	Jerky
Placer Mountain	8,928	Ortiz
Apache Mountain	8,920	(Apache Natl. For.)
Little Squaretop	8,919	Organ
Lookout Mountain	8,872	Black
Organ Peak	8,870	Organ
John Kerr Peak	8,862	Long Canyon
West Mountain	8,842	Capitan
Laughlin Peak	8,836	(Northeast N. M.)
Bay Buck Peak	8,825	San Mateo
Church Mountain	8,805	Sierra Blanca
Chuska Peak	8,795	Chuska
Dead Man Peak	8,786	(N.-cen. N. M.)
South Mountain	8,748	(Albuquerque Rgn.)
Dillon Mountain	8,740	(Apache Natl. For.)
Guadalupe Mountain	8,735	Taos
Sierra Grande	8,720	(Northeast N. M.)
Bearhead Peak	8,711	Jemez
Granite Peak	8,699	Diablo
Palomas Peak	8,685	Sandia
Pinon Knob	8,677	(Gila Natl. For.)
Oscura Peak	8,640	Oscura
Gallinas Peak	8,637	(Corona Region)
Cooney Peak	8,600	Mogollon
Zilditloi Mountain	8,573	Chuska
Clara Peak	8,549	Jemez
Animas Peak	8,519	Animas
Patos Mountain	8,508	Sacaramento
St. Peters Dome	8,463	Jemez

Baldy Peak	8,445	Organ
San Francisco Mountains	8,435	San Francisco
Cooks Peak	8,404	Cooks
Cerro Blanco	8,388	Manzano
Big Hatchet Peak	8,366	Big Hatchet
Twin Sisters	8,340	Pinos Altos
Tucson Mountain	8,308	Sacramento
Devisadero Peak	8,300	Taos
Squaretop	8,300	Organ
Wedge	8,300	Organ
San Pedro Mountain	8,242	San Pedro
San Andres Peak	8,239	San Andres
Oro Quay Peak	8,226	San Pedro
Capulin Mountain	8,215	(Northeast N. M.)
Saddle Mountain	8,200	San Francisco
Bearsprings Peak	8,195	Jemez
Boundary Peak	8,182	Jemez
Magdalena Peak	8,152	Magdalena
Middle Rabbit Ear	8,150	Organ
Hellroaring Mesa	8,145	(Apache Natl. For.)
East Carrizo Cone	8,128	Sacaramento
Boiler Peak	8,048	Black
Burro Peak	8,035	Burro
Rabbit Ear Plateau	8,010	Organ
Greer Peak	8,005	San Andres
Cabezon	8,000	(West-cen. N. M.)
North Oscura Peak	7,999	Oscura
Jacks Mountain	7,986	Burro
Hart Peak	7,978	Cimarron
Thompson Cone	7,932	Black
Haystack Mountain	7,871	Black
Seventy-four Mountain	7,818	Mogollon
Vera Cruz Mountain	7,800	Sacramento
A Four Mountain	7,770	Pinos Altos
Cedro Peak	7,767	Manzanita
Baylor Peak	7,721	Organ

Mount Washington	7,716	Manzanita
Kelly Mountains	7,650	Kelly
Guaje Mountain	7,636	Jemez
Monte Largo	7,606	(Albuquerque Rgn.)
Saliz Mountains	7,576	Saliz
Sol se Mete	7,541	Manzanita
Whiteface Mountain	7,530	Los Pinos
Reading Mountain	7,490	Pinos Altos
Cerro Pelon	7,470	Manzanita
Huerfano Peak	7,470	(Northwest N. M.)
Niggerhead	7,400	Gallinas
Emery Peak	7,350	(Folsom Region)
Gillespie Mountain	7,309	Animas
Timber Mountain	7,300	Caballo
Polvadera Mountain	7,292	Lemitar
Baxter Mountain	7,285	Sacramento
Wind Mountain	7,280	Cornudas
Cerro Montosa	7,259	Los Pinos
Socorro Peak	7,243	Socorro
Shiprock	7,178	(Northwest N.M.)
Capitol Peak	7,098	San Andres
Cerro Bonanza	7,088	(Cerillos Region)
Bullard Peak	7,064	Big Burro
Bear Peak	7,055	San Andres
Starvation Peak	7,042	Las Vegas
San Augustin	7,025	Organ
Center Peak	7,020	Animas
North Baylor Peak	7,018	Organ
Strawberry Peak	7,012	Lemitar
Table Mountain	7,000	Gallinas
Angels Peak	6,988	(Bloomfield Rgn.)
Gym Peak	6,750	Florida
Devoy's Peak	6,740	(Northeast N. M.)
Alamo Mountain	6,670	Cornudas
Knight Peak	6,602	Big Burro
Sierra de las Uvas	6,601	(Hatch Region)

Hachita Peak	6,585	Little Hatchet
Black Point	6,467	Peloncillo
Guadalupe Mountain	6,450	Peloncillo
Bald Mountain	6,396	Little Burro
Schoolhouse Mountain	6,370	Big Burro
Bunk Robinson Peak	6,241	Peloncillo
Flying W Mountain	6,217	Cedar Mountain
Cedar Mountain	6,207	Cedar Mountain
Caballo Cone	6,091	Caballo
Wildhorse Peak	6,078	Big Burro
North Pyramid Peak	6,002	Pyramid
Caballo Mountain	5,993	Caballo
Hilo Peak	5,955	Animas
Rabbit Ear Mountain	5,940	(Northeast N. M.)
Mount Riley	5,915	Potrillo
South Pyramid Peak	5,910	Pyramid
Doña Ana Peak	5,899	Doña Ana
Robledo Mountain	5,876	Picacho-Robledo
Rimrock Mountain	5,785	Pyramid
Cornudas Mountain	5,730	Cornudas
Little Black Peak	5,679	(Carrizozo Rgn.)
Goat Mountain	5,607	Pyramid
Bishop Cap	5,419	(Las Cruces Rgn.)
North Anthonys Nose	5,368	Franklin
Kirk Peak	5,359	Pyramid
Eighty-five Hill	5,105	Pyramid
Aberdeen Peak	5,044	Pyramid
Lee Peak	5,022	Pyramid
Niggerhead	4,993	Pyramid
Tucumcari Mountain	4,967	(Tucumcari Rgn.)
Picacho Peak	4,954	Picacho-Robledo
Swallow Fork Peak	4,954	Pyramid
Tortugas Mountain	4,931	(Las Cruces Rgn.)
Cedar Knob	4,902	Pyramid
Dogs Head	4,812	Pyramid
Guzmans Lookout Mountain	4,762	Potrillo

SUBJECT INDEX